Mentoring Across Boundaries

Helping Beginning Teachers Succeed in Challenging Situations

Jean Boreen and Donna Niday

with Mary K. Johnson

Stenhouse Publishers
Portland, Maine

Stenhouse Publishers
www.stenhouse.com

Library of Congress Cataloging-in-Publication Data
Boreen, Jean
    Mentoring across boundaries : helping beginning teachers succeed in challenging situations / Jean Boreen and Donna Niday with Mary K. Johnson.
    p. cm.
    Includes bibliographical references.
    ISBN 1-57110-377-5 (alk. paper)
    1. Mentoring in education. 2. Teachers—In-service training. I. Niday, Donna. II. Johnson, Mary K. III. Title.
LB1731.4.B67 2003
370'.71'5—dc21   2003050692

Cover photographs by Donna Niday (*top:* Amanda Cooper Stewart and Michelle Tremmel, Iowa State Unversity, Ames, Iowa; *middle:* Kathryn Wenck and Kris Magel, Ames Middle School, Ames, Iowa; *bottom:* Denise Biechler and Mark Willard, Roland-Story High School, Story City, Iowa)

Manufactured in the United States of America on acid-free paper
09 08 07 06 05   9 8 7 6 5 4 3 2

To the mentors who share so much of their time, commitment, and enthusiasm working with beginning teachers

Contents

Foreword

One of the truths of my teaching life has been feeling the need to apologize to former students. I underestimated the complexity of teaching early in my career, and that showed up in the choices I made and the well-intentioned missteps I took as a novice teacher. The same can safely be said of learning to become a good mentor. Across my teaching life, I became (or was assigned to be) the unofficial or official mentor to seventeen student teachers and numerous early-career teachers. In my City High School classroom, I greeted teacher candidates from the university as "guests" who were allowed to borrow my students for a short time. I wasn't particularly helpful, I'm sure, primarily because I wasn't sure *how* to help. As a very young department chair, I was thrust into a situation of advising newcomers about teaching without knowing what I should be looking for or how to communicate constructive criticism. I'm struck by the need to apologize for the way I defined and enacted the mentoring role when I first took it on.

In the early days, I offered a brand of "feel good" mentoring that extended emotional support and comfort to the novice teachers assigned to me. I was focused on easing the entry into teaching rather than furthering new teachers' learning about how to confront difficult problems in their practice. I'm sure I did not help them view their teaching as a site for learning, nor did I offer specific feedback about their individual accomplishments rather than general praise for a job well done. Nonetheless, my role seemed important to all the stakeholders. After all, I was doing a service to the profession. The novice teachers felt all warm and fuzzy. The administration could say they had a supportive, well-conceived induction plan. I felt good about nurturing new teachers. No problem.

Which brings me back to the core of my apology to my early mentees. I'm really sorry. I know I provided support—but not challenge. Or at least not enough challenge to call what I did "educative" mentoring. It took years for me to redefine my role as mentor. Only when I sought out other teachers who would talk about their mentoring experiences—teachers who would question the goals of mentoring relationships and explore the dilemmas they had encountered—was I able to reconceptualize what a mentor could *do*. With clearer purposes for mentoring, I learned to find openings for fruitful talk that could lead to a productive line of thinking with a mentee. I pushed novice colleagues to pinpoint their problems in the classroom to help them talk about teaching in more precise and analytic ways. I no longer settled for "Things aren't going well," or "The kids were awful today." I redirected the mentee's focus to student learning and away from teacher performance. I modeled an inquiry approach to my own learning and reinforced theoretical ideas in context in an effort to help novices develop useful knowledge and principled understanding. I sought to become a living example of one person's approach to teaching, making public my struggles and giving voice to my wonderings about how to "do it better."

But each mentoring relationship posed a distinctly new challenge and required a different set of considerations on my part; I could have used more help in addressing many uncertainties. For example, I was unsure about how to ask building administrators and university partners for assistance or how to counsel a teacher who was clearly headed for burnout. I stewed over how to talk to my male mentees in productive ways and how to sustain a mentoring relationship with past student teachers and colleagues who had moved on to other settings.

The authors of *Mentoring Across Boundaries* have firsthand knowledge of the dilemmas mentors face. They offer scenarios that will help mentors imagine how they might broach difficult problems with their mentees and anticipate future obstacles. This is an important book, a book built on the premise that a mentor can have a lasting positive influence on the careers of newcomers to teaching. Accomplished mentoring depends on *learning* to mentor, though, and I believe the authors have made a substantial contribution to that literature.

Margaret Graham

Acknowledgments

We would like to thank the following people for reading the manuscript and offering suggestions: Sibylle Gruber (for exceptional assistance), Cynthia Kosso, Laura Gray-Rosendale, Ruth Ann Van Donslear, Joe Potts, Bob Tremmel, and Jeff Johnson.

Thanks to the many mentors and beginning teachers who allowed us to work with and interview them for various chapters throughout this book. This book could not exist without them.

We would like to thank Sandra Raymond, Rob Petrone, Sarah Brown Wessling, and Susan Kimball for writing large portions of Chapters 5 and 8.

We also express appreciation to the folks at Stenhouse, especially Bill Varner, Philippa Stratton, Tom Seavey, Brenda Power, and Martha Drury for helping us attempt and complete this project.

In addition, we thank the numerous mentors in the public schools with whom we have worked over the years; the Ames Community School BEST Team in Ames, Iowa, as well as teachers in the Flagstaff Unified School District in Flagstaff, Arizona, receive special thanks. Their example has helped us formulate the philosophical stances we illustrate throughout this book.

Our family and friends have also contributed to this text: John, Amanda, and Laura Boreen; Ruth Ann and Norman Van Donslear; Leila Niday; Nancy, Ronnie, Jason, and Chris Roberts; and Jeff, Liz, Andrew, Matt, and Joe Johnson.

Introduction

At a recent educational conference on mentoring issues, a colleague shared an increasingly common story. In his rural district, it has become more difficult to retain new teachers. This is not because their students are exceptionally difficult or because the pay is below average, for neither of these things is true. He identified the problem as the rural setting itself. "We try to be friendly and to include new teachers in social events and community life. The problem is that there *isn't* enough community life for young, single professionals, especially if they come to us from an urban setting."

Although we speak and write frequently about mentoring issues, this was one we hadn't previously considered. After the conference, we began to contemplate additional mentoring issues that have not been widely discussed. What concerns are unique to urban settings, for example? How do we support beginning teachers who work in alternative schools for at-risk students? Considering these questions led us to even more basic matters: how age, gender, or cultural differences may complicate the mentoring process. As we began to talk to more of our friends and colleagues, we realized that these issues permeate our schools and thus our professional lives in a variety of combinations and with varying intensity. And as we consider the fluid nature of these issues across the various boundaries of school life, we must further complicate our discussion of mentoring. Mentoring becomes more, then, than a veteran teacher supporting a beginning teacher; for many involved in this type of relationship, it provides a vast array of life and professional learning experiences that enhance their ability to interact with their colleagues in a collegial manner.

In our previous book, *Mentoring Beginning Teachers: Guiding, Reflecting, Coaching,* we offer recommendations for a variety of elementary and secondary situations. In this text, *Mentoring Across Boundaries,* we explore many of the specific issues that affect the mentoring relationship. Once again, this text is designed for mentors working with either student teachers or beginning colleagues. We have also included sections pertinent to administrators interested in securing quality mentoring relationships for their faculty.

In the first section, "Setting the Stage for Effective Mentoring," we examine what it takes to be a mentor and how administrators and university colleagues can support mentors. We also discuss the importance of goal setting for both mentors and beginning teachers.

The second section, "Responding to Challenging Situations," focuses on some of the conditions within mentoring relationships that create additional anxiety. The influence of age, gender, and ethnicity on mentoring relationships is considered. This is followed by a look at the problems faced by those supporting beginning teachers in rural and urban schools, mentoring for veteran teachers who move into new school environments, and encouraging those teachers who work with at-risk students. Another issue is the mentorship of teachers whose devotion to their demanding role has begun to produce burnout, followed by a consideration of the benefits of self-mentoring when traditional mentoring is not available. We next move into the area of remediation for teachers who are failing in the eyes of their colleagues and administrators; this is an extremely sensitive area, yet no aspect of mentoring is potentially more rewarding and necessary. Finally, we consider how mentoring through technology can provide a variety of benefits to both beginning and veteran teachers. Each of these chapters considers both potential difficulties and opportunities created as new teachers and their mentors adjust to these factors.

The most recent report from the National Commission on Teaching and America's Future on the teacher shortage says, "The conventional wisdom is that we can't find enough good teachers. The truth is that we can't keep enough good teachers" (January 29, 2003). The report goes on to say that the actual problem is more directly related to teacher retention. NCTAF reports that:

> *according to a new report about the nation's teacher supply crisis, "No Dream Denied: A Pledge to America's Children," . . . almost a third of all new teachers*

leave the classroom after three years, and close to 50 percent leave after five years. The report finds that retirement isn't the main culprit; teachers who leave the classroom for reasons other than retirement outnumber those retiring by almost three to one. More than a quarter of a million teachers stop teaching every year; the cumulative effect is that high teacher turnover and attrition are undermining teaching quality.

All of us in education are familiar with these types of reports on attrition rates for new professionals: 250,000 people leaving the profession each year, with many of them citing poor pay, isolation, and lack of parent and administrative support. We cannot afford to allow this trend to continue. Mentoring has been proven to be one of the most effective approaches in keeping teachers in the field. As we noted in Chapter 2 of *Mentoring Beginning Teachers,*

> *mentoring reduces attrition by one-half or more. Sandra Odell (1992) found that the attrition rate for teachers receiving one year of mentoring was only 16 percent after four years of teaching, about half the national attrition rate. In fact, 80 percent of the teachers who had received mentoring predicted they would still be teaching in ten years.*
>
> *Odell's results reinforce the findings of other studies, which indicate that the first year of teaching seems to have greater correlation to teacher retention than either prior academic performance or the quality of the teacher preparation program. (p. 7)*

All of these moves are important measures in the growing awareness that we must all work to keep talented educators in the field. We hope this book encourages you to consider your own role as a mentor and colleague, whatever your situation, and to take a more active approach to working with new teachers in your district.

PART

I

Setting the Stage
for Effective Mentoring

Choosing and Supporting Good Mentors

Luke, an established mentor teacher, had a suggestion for us. After reading *Mentoring Beginning Teachers: Guiding, Reflecting, Coaching,* he encouraged us to write to administrators and university placement offices, exhorting them to carefully select both the schools and the teachers who would be the cooperating or mentor teachers. As Luke points out,

> There are some, I'm afraid, who do not possess the combination of talent, experience, judgment, and generosity of spirit required to guide a young teacher appropriately . . . the receiving school should have a check list by which they choose the master teacher, and I think that for a university to accept without question a school administration's judgment is doing so at their peril.

We absolutely agree with Luke that many problems experienced by student or beginning teachers could be avoided with a more careful matching of mentors to new teachers. However, many schools have policies that assign mentor responsibilities to their teachers based upon years of experience, rotation, or simple convenience. This approach typically leads to mediocre to poor experiences for student and beginning teachers within the mentoring relationship. Why? Because a mentor who is not personally invested in the mentoring relationship will not provide the kind of support a beginning teacher needs to grow in the profession. For example, we know of a high school where the university liaison, a faculty member at the high school paid by the university to help facilitate the placement process, walks up and down the halls yelling out, "We've got a history student teacher who needs a placement; anybody want him?" This school has gotten mixed reviews from many student teachers. One noted,

> *My mentor teacher just wanted someone to do his work for him; I didn't learn anything from him about teaching except how to use the Xerox machine so I could crank out an endless supply of worksheets. There was nothing he did for or with me that confirmed my desire to be a teacher. It was my conversations with another teacher, a newer teacher to the district, that kept me focused on teaching. And she can't even get a student teacher because she hasn't been here long enough to get into the rotation.*

This story and too many others like it led us to follow Luke's suggestion and provide a kind of "how to" for choosing strong mentors. In this chapter, we address what administrators should look for in a successful mentor, the responsibilities administrators have after the mentoring placement is made, and university responsibilities concerning the preparation of and support for mentors and beginning teachers during their teaching careers.

Sarah was a veteran teacher with ten years of solid service as a sixth-grade teacher. Known for her creativity in curriculum planning and high standards for her students, Sarah was held in high esteem by parents. Her colleagues, while respecting the strong educator Sarah was, did not find her an easy associate with whom to work. Her inability to listen to others' suggestions and her tendency to take over meetings left Sarah's colleagues feeling frustrated and annoyed. Sarah was oblivious to this, and when she was once again passed over for a student teacher, she felt compelled to talk to her principal, Ted.

"I've been wondering," she began, "why I haven't been asked to take a student teacher or to mentor one of my newer colleagues. Diana, the other sixth-grade teacher, has had several student teachers, and she mentored Elizabeth when she came in last year. I've been in the district as long as Diana has, and my teaching evaluations are just as good. What am I missing?"

Ted looked uncomfortable as he responded. "Don't take it personally, Sarah. You are a great teacher. There's no question about that. However, we don't assign the mentorship of new or student teachers by turn. It's a matchmaking process, and so far, we haven't had an applicant who we thought would benefit from your style of teaching or mentorship. Also, to be honest, we haven't been sure you'd be comfortable sharing your classroom with a rookie."

"Well, that's probably true to some degree," Sarah said, "but I still would like the opportunity to try. And if we're being honest, I wonder what others think about the fact that you haven't assigned me a student or a new teacher while Diana gets so many. Will they think I'm not as good a teacher as Diana? Or not as professional?"

It isn't easy to explain to teachers like Sarah why they may not be suited to mentoring a beginning teacher. Yet we applaud Ted's courage in deciding to assign new teachers to mentors based on their solid mentoring abilities— which is discussed in the next section of this chapter—rather than on years of service. Ted apparently realizes that Sarah is possessive of her classroom, her students, and her pedagogical choices. He may also have observed her somewhat rigid interactions with colleagues at staff meetings or her defensiveness when parents question her practice. Sarah is a successful teacher, but she may not have the flexibility needed to be a successful mentor.

Being asked to mentor is not something a teacher should automatically expect. Mentoring assignments are not a type of "merit" award, nor are they a recognition of seniority. There is a regrettable tendency within some school districts to assign mentoring by turn: this semester it's Diana's turn to be mentor, next time it's Sarah's. Although this appears equitable, it is actually a poor mentoring practice unless both teachers have the qualities necessary to mentor successfully. Both administrators and teachers need to understand that mentoring should not be seen as competitive. It's not a criticism when a student teacher is assigned to someone else. It's also no great honor to be chosen for these roles. It is simply a recognition that a specific teacher meets the "job description."

Qualities Administrators Should Seek in Mentor Teachers

What are the qualities of strong mentor teachers? From our work with successful mentor educators, we would say that they

- have mastered the basic skills of teaching,
- understand the need for flexibility, in attitude and in practice,
- accept the possibility that pedagogical styles other than the ones they use may be successful,

- realize that possessiveness of students and classroom policies is detrimental to a mentoring relationship,

- can confront troublesome situations as necessary, and

- have a professional vision beyond their own classroom.

Mastery of Basic Teaching Skills

Ted looked around Diana's room appreciatively. A poster on the front wall of the room clearly explained her management expectations for her sixth-grade students. More posters outlining how to use the six traits in writing and showing the rotation of the solar system provided a glimpse into some of Diana's current units of instruction. Ted had heard glowing reports from his secretary as well as parents about how organized Diana was and what a joy it was to work with someone who was so specific in her expectations for students and parents alike. Ted appreciated the fact that so many of his teachers were solid in a variety of ways, but he knew that with Diana, his school had a teacher who knew her content and managed to interact with parents, students, and administrators in the most professional manner possible.

In this example, we see Diana embodying the traits of a teacher who has mastered her profession. These include content competence, successful classroom management skills, and organizational abilities (daily tasks, student records, and management of classroom materials). If teachers have difficulties in any of these areas, they should not be considered as potential mentors. Too often, administrators' interactions with teachers are limited to faculty meetings, extracurricular activities, or chats in the hallway. These contacts are important but do not reveal the teacher's skills in these areas. Therefore, it is imperative that administrators be in classrooms often enough to be able to assess these basic skills before selecting mentors. It is impossible to make the most successful matches without this knowledge.

Flexibility in Attitude and in Practice

Carolyn, an art teacher for a number of years, looked at the lesson plan in front of her with an approving smile. "Your planning is so good, Kelsie. You really seem to have taken to heart my comments on timing for activities versus direct instruction. And I'm also glad you went ahead and incorporated the lit circles over the author biographies into your unit. When you were first talking about having the kids discuss artists in small groups, I have to admit I thought you were trying too hard to be interdisciplinary. But the way you've explained it in your rationale—why you think the students are served by having some insights into the lives and cultural contexts of some of their favorite artists—well, you've sold me. I'm really eager to see how the kids respond."

Flexibility is one of the most important keys to effective mentoring. Whether we are considering flexibility in terms of the pedagogical choices a teacher makes or considering how they respond to the various organizational problems that occur during the average class day, we know that the ability to adjust to meet a variety of situations is paramount in the successful mentor. The manner in which a mentor shows her flexibility may not always be obvious. In the above example, Carolyn praises the flexibility her student teacher has shown even as she remarks on her own change of heart concerning the use of literature circles in an art classroom. Carolyn's approach is subtle but positive, modeling for her mentee the need for flexibility and how developing that understanding may be part of a process.

Acceptance of the Possibility That Other Pedagogical Styles May Be Successful

Leo, who has been teaching science at the middle school level for twelve years, was happy to meet his first student teacher, Steve. He generously shared all of his unit plans, including handouts, quizzes, and vocabulary pages. Steve accepted these resources, but used them and other materials to create a unit of his own. Watching Steve teach a few days later, Leo realized that Steve was not following the original unit. Leo felt offended by what he considered Steve's rejection of his successful teaching materials, a reaction that was not lessened by the fact that Steve's unit appeared to be equally successful. He questioned Steve in front of the students and insisted that Steve return to his materials. Eventually, the university supervisor and building principal persuaded Leo to allow Steve to try various techniques, but Leo never felt quite comfortable when Steve did so.

There are many ways to teach well; individual teaching personalities can differ widely and still offer students excellent opportunities to learn and grow. Perfect matches between mentors and new professionals rarely happen; however, mentors comfortable with their own style should be able to accept different approaches without being threatened or feeling the need to be unduly critical. One common difficulty that arises is when the mentor teacher is unable to accept the possibility that other pedagogical styles may ultimately be successful.

Whereas Leo felt possessive of his carefully crafted teaching materials, other teachers find themselves reacting negatively when the regard of their students begins to shift to the student teacher, however temporarily.

Possessiveness of Students and Classroom Policies Can Be Detrimental

Sharon, a university supervisor, looked over the list of teachers with whom she could place her history education students for their fieldwork experience. She frowned slightly when she got to Joan's name. Joan was spectacularly successful with her Advanced Placement history students. Because she recognized Joan's professional achievements with her high school students, Sharon had, in previous semesters, assigned student teachers to her. However, none of the three had been entirely successful in Joan's classroom. Each of the student teaching experiences started well, but at the point when the student teacher began to demonstrate competence, independence, and positive interactions with students, Joan had, according to all three student teachers, subtly undermined their progress. In a process with which Sharon had become all too familiar, Joan would first criticize lesson plans—unfairly, according to the beginning teacher. Next, she would interrupt the student teacher when lessons were in progress, often giving contradictory information to the students. Eventually, the student teacher's confidence was sufficiently eroded so that he or she was unable to perform as well as would normally be expected. After hearing a number of complaints from the student teachers, Sharon began dropping subtle hints and finally, made direct suggestions to Joan. These had little effect, however, because Joan insisted that she was only acting in the best interest of both the secondary students and her student teachers. In essence, the issue does not really stem from the student teachers. It is Joan's issue. She does not want to acknowledge the possibility that the novice may eventually be a rival for her strong performance in the classroom. In a sense, she is possessive of both her students and her position in the classroom.

It is a source of frustration to both the university supervisor and the building administrator that such a competent and exciting teacher cannot serve as a mentor. However, Joan's possessiveness has negatively affected three very good candidates. Despite her professional success in other areas, she should not receive further placements. However, if a seniority system were in place, Joan would be allowed to take her turn with others—and this could spell disaster for future student teachers. For this reason, we do not support the concept of mentorship-by-turns. Only teachers with appropriate mentoring skills should be allowed to act as mentors.

Confronting Troublesome Situations as Necessary

Unlike Joan, Alice is determined never to cause her student teachers to feel uncomfortable in her classroom. Her hesitation stems from her inability to confront her student teachers as needed. All of us, of course, have been conditioned to be polite and respectful of others; none of us is completely comfortable with confrontation. However, successful mentors must be willing to overcome this discomfort and address any problems that arise.

Alice was very pleased to have been assigned Patrick as a student teacher. He seemed to fit in well in her festive yet orderly third-grade classroom, and she quickly provided him with a number of resources to use for planning his lessons. After a few weeks, Alice noticed that Patrick was coming to class unprepared. Because he was so bright and knowledgeable about his content, the lessons were still adequate; however, Alice could look ahead and predict that later lessons would be impossible without stronger preparation. Yet Patrick seemed proud of what he was accomplishing. Concerned, Alice went to Frank, a longtime colleague.

"I don't want to offend Patrick, so I haven't said anything, but I really feel there's trouble ahead. What should I do?"

"You've got to be honest with him, Alice," replied Frank. "If you don't, he's going to keep planning and teaching in the same manner, and next year, when he's on his own, he's certain to have problems."

"But what if he gets upset with me? I'm not dissatisfied with him in other ways."

"Alice, he's a *student* teacher. He's here to learn, and you've accepted the responsibility of teaching him. With that comes the expectation that you may have to correct poor practice. In the end, he'll be glad you did."

Patrick listened to Alice's concerns about this lack of preparation. "I'm really glad you shared this with me. I don't want to do anything that would hurt the kids. You know, Alice, you need to be more honest with me about things I'm not doing well. Sometimes I can tell you're unhappy with something I've done, but you never tell me why. When I ask you directly for feedback, you always say, 'No, no, it's fine' when obviously it really hasn't been. You don't know how frustrating this is for me."

Alice was initially taken aback by Patrick's comments. Because she has such a gentle and polite spirit, she had rarely encountered criticism of her own practice. Instead of getting angry, however, Alice used Patrick's comments to improve her mentoring skills. She realized that both Patrick and Frank were right to encourage her to be more assertive. In this way, Alice was markedly different from Joan, who refused to accept the possibility that she was to blame for any problems in the mentoring relationship. Therefore, Alice will probably continue to be a solid mentor, whereas Joan will no longer have opportunities to work with beginning teachers.

A Professional Vision Beyond the Classroom

To be successful, mentors must take an interest in the wider professional world. For example, compare Terry and Maxine.

Terry, a successful mentor, attends and presents at professional conferences at both state and national levels. The National Council of Teachers of Math Web site is bookmarked on his computer, and he regularly joins in the conversations on the council's professional listserv. Because of these contacts, he is able to introduce beginning teachers to the exciting world of research and professional interaction, which they might be slow to discover on their own. Terry's professional vision enhances his interactions with beginning teachers and colleagues alike.

Although Terry's colleague Maxine has been an effective mentor for beginning teachers in many ways, she limits her influence to classroom practice. She is not involved in professional organizations or conferences and does not read professional journals. Consequently, she is unable to foster further professional growth with the teachers she mentors. Maxine is not modeling a professional vision, but more important, she is not introducing young teachers to the resources that could support them when their time with a mentor is finished.

Does this mean that Maxine should not be assigned to mentor a new teacher? Possibly. More important, it means that Maxine's district should be doing all it can to promote and encourage both new and experienced teachers to be involved with their professional organizations. Some school districts actually require all their teachers to affiliate with at least one professional organization. An even better practice is to allow teachers both time and substitute coverage to attend and/or present at conferences. If money for conference attendance is not an option, teachers should at least be encouraged to consider on-line mentoring (discussed in detail in Chapter 11). Administrators and school districts can also recognize teachers who participate in these types of professional opportunities through career ladder points or steps on the pay scale to further promote teacher enthusiasm for these activities.

Administrative Responsibilities

Administrators are key to helping secure positive mentoring relationships for both veteran and beginning teachers. Specifically, they need to

- spend considerable time watching their teachers teach,
- observe the mentoring relationship from its inception,
- analyze teaching situations that may be unsuitable for a mentoring placement, and
- change mentoring relationships if necessary.

Spending Time Watching Teachers Teach

Although it is often difficult to find the time to observe teachers, it is less time-consuming in the long run than having to rehire teachers on a regular basis. Firsthand administrative knowledge of teachers' strengths and weaknesses is a good investment. If the administrator in charge of personnel has too large a staff for extensive one-on-one contact, it is imperative that he or she assign senior teachers or department chairs to fulfill this task. Mentoring placements should never be made randomly, by turn, or on casual recommendations from students or colleagues. Rather, they should be made on the basis of knowledgeable observation and extended conversations with the teachers involved.

Observing the Mentoring Relationship from Its Inception

Again, a senior teacher or department chair may carry out the actual observations, but responsible administrators should remain informed and be willing to commend or intervene as needed. Many mentoring placements have little oversight from the cooperating schools once they have been established. The university supervisor provides support in the case of student teachers, but beginning teacher/mentor teacher pairings may receive little support. Often, the knowledge that someone else is overseeing the relationship provides both relief and accountability.

Recognizing Teaching Situations That May Be Unsuitable for a Mentoring Placement

Nathan shows great promise as a mentor, but this semester, he is teaching four sections of a pilot course on the history of technological innovations. Nathan's expertise in history and computer information systems makes this class a sensible and interesting offering for him and his students; however, it would be highly unlikely for the university to have a student teacher qualified to teach such a course. In our local district, one very competent potential mentor has one content course in English and two elective courses in dance each semester. As much as we admire her work, it would be difficult to place a student teacher in this situation because of state and university requirements.

Another red flag situation might involve class size. Student teachers are sometimes assigned to teachers who have extremely large classes in the hope that the extra pair of hands will alleviate the consequences of the overcrowding. However, this is unfair and problematic in the sense that the student teacher often has limited opportunities to teach independently in this setting.

Splitting the student teacher's time between two mentor teachers is frequently suggested as a solution to some of the above situations. We do not recommend this practice, because it makes unusually heavy demands on the student teacher. Because of differences in management styles, content coverage, and student load, the student teacher may be overwhelmed. It is difficult enough for a student teacher to follow the lead or direction of one teacher; it is unrealistic to expect an optimal result when two mentors have differing expectations. Likewise, beginning teachers should not be assigned two mentors. Their differing viewpoints and suggestions may confuse rather than clarify those difficult first years.

Changing Mentoring Relationships If Necessary

Administrators who have followed all of the above suggestions may still find themselves dealing with relationships that do not work. We address some specific examples of this in other chapters of this book; the important message here is to change the mentor relationship if it's not working for the people involved. Yes, this may take a lot of subtlety on the part of the administrator. Both members of the relationship must understand that although each did his or her best, the mentoring is not working for any number of reasons, and these may be beyond anyone's control. The administrator must also keep track of why the relationship didn't work. Was the mentor too inflexible? Was the mentee unwilling to challenge herself to make necessary changes? Did a difference in gender cause difficulty in the relationship? This awareness will help with mentor pairings down the road.

Perhaps the most underused resource in the mentoring paradigm is the university supervisor. At most universities, the university supervisor teaches methods courses or advises majors in their field as well as supervises student teachers. Although it is more common for university supervisors to offer recommendations regarding student teaching placements, they are equally good resources for districts that have hired their recent graduates and intend to place them in mentoring relationships. They know the potential professional capabilities of their students very well. In addition, because they have interacted with veteran teachers during student teaching supervisions or through professional gatherings, they often have a good sense of the strengths of veteran teachers across a number of schools or even districts. This knowledge enables them to make helpful recommendations to administrators. Much beneficial information can be quickly and informally shared during the placement process. Those administrators who have come to rely on university supervisor recommendations often find their mentoring placements more successful. Those administrators who do not seek this input seem to encounter more difficulties that too often result in having to change mentor pairings well into the school year, and this is not beneficial to the beginning or the veteran teacher.

University Responsibilities

Finally, what should universities do to make sure they are supporting mentoring relationships? They must

- prepare student teachers realistically for classroom life,
- build bridges with schools, and
- encourage professional development.

Preparing Student Teachers

University education programs must strive to provide students with an accurate view of classroom life. It is easy for university instructors to focus too heavily on pedagogical philosophy and neglect the practical aspects of teaching. Teacher education programs that consistently employ instructors and professors who have little or no actual K–12 teaching experience or for whom that experience is many years in the past are particularly prone to this failing. There are two solutions to this problem. The first is to employ university-level educators with recent and extensive K–12 experience; the second is to get the preservice teachers into classrooms early and often. Also, conversations with practicing teachers and readings from teacher-written materials can support both university courses and inservice programs for new professionals. These contextualized "teacher stories" often provide that dose of reality that idealistic young teachers need to balance the philosophical with the practical.

Building Bridges with Schools

Universities should also work to establish sound bridges between themselves and the schools with which they work. These bridges are important to teacher education programs in developing professional relationships with teachers and administrators for a number of reasons. The more the university programs can count on consistent mentoring and support within each school in a district, the easier it is for university supervisors and placement directors to make student teaching placements that work. For example, a university might offer mentor meetings or training for those teachers interested in becoming mentors. Recently, area teachers gathered at our university for a workshop on successful mentoring practices. The university provided the meeting space, a complimentary copy of a text on successful mentoring, and a luncheon for attendees. One teacher noted, "Not only is this a great opportunity for those of us in the public schools to get together outside of school, but it gives us a chance to touch base with university faculty to understand the teacher preparation program better. It also gives us a chance to offer education faculty some suggestions on what we'd like to see them provide to preservice teachers before they come to us as student teachers."

Another way of establishing a support for schools is to connect the resources of the university to public school teachers. The recent visit of a prominent author to our university was the occasion for such support. Faculty members familiar with that author's work offered a Saturday workshop for area teachers a month before the author arrived. The workshop focused on how three different university faculty members had used the author's works in their own classrooms, then suggested short readings by the author that were suitable for high school students and explained major themes in the author's work. This allowed the area teachers to prepare their students more fully for the author's visit to the schools and strengthened relationships between individual teachers and university faculty members who shared their interests. A situation like this provides not only a resource for area schools, but also a much-needed opportunity for professional collaboration and conversation between the two groups of educators. Too often, high school teachers complain that they have no way of knowing what college professors expect students to know; university faculty members complain that high school teachers don't do enough to prepare students for college. Obviously, situations where the two groups can converse can be an important step in opening stronger lines of communication so that each group is better prepared to strengthen their students' education.

Encouraging Professional Development

The university should also encourage the professional development of practicing teachers. One practical way to do this is to encourage districts to extend career ladder credit as part of the compensation for mentoring a student or beginning teacher in addition to university incentives. Another supportive position is to offer courses of particular interest to teachers at "teacher-friendly" times each semester and during the summer. Providing university credit for mentor training like that discussed above should also be considered.

Sabbatical opportunities in which teachers from the public schools are encouraged to accept adjunct positions in teacher preparation programs for one semester or one year clearly benefit both the university and the public schools. The public school teachers gain exposure to the newest information and current trends in the teaching of their subject area. They also have the opportunity to observe their colleagues' classrooms as they supervise student teachers or participate in university outreach programs. Preservice teachers benefit from the immediate experience and relevance of courses taught by these successful educators.

As we finish this chapter, we should note once again that as educators, we should look at mentoring situations as opportunities to support all involved in, possibly, a new type of lifelong learning. Working at odds, even if it is not intended, potentially creates more problems for beginning teachers; working together provides a richer teaching environment for all of us.

Summary

Mentoring relationships are important in keeping beginning teachers in the profession. School administrators need to be more active in the manner in which they choose mentors. First, they must consider the qualities of strong mentor teachers: (1) mastery of the basic skills of teaching; (2) an understanding of the need for flexibility, in attitude and in practice; (3) an ability to confront troublesome situations as necessary; and (4) a professional vision beyond his or her own classroom. In addition, school administrators must take an active interest in the mentoring process as it unfolds. This means that they need to spend time watching their teachers teach, observe the mentoring relationship on more than one occasion and in a variety of contexts, consider which teaching situations may be unsuitable for a mentoring placement, and change the mentor pairing if necessary. Universities may also help make the mentoring situation more successful by preparing student teachers for classroom life in a realistic manner, building bridges with schools to ensure that professional conversations occur between the two levels, and encouraging professional development in beginning and mentor teachers as a way of supporting the field well into the future. Following these approaches can help secure more beneficial relationships for all involved.

Web Sites Featuring Teacher Stories

Teacher Stories

www.studentsasresearchers.nexus.edu.au/learning/teachers/teachstories.html

The Teacher Laptop Foundation

www.teacherlaptop.com/teacherstories.html

Teacher Tales

www.teachertales.com/default.html

Teacher Testimony

www.4teachers.org/testimony

Books Featuring Teacher Stories

Ayers, William, and Gloria Ladson-Billings. 2001. *To Teach: The Journey of a Teacher.* New York: Teachers College Press.

Canfield, Jack, Mark Victor Hansen, and Sharon J. Wohlmuth. 2003. *Chicken Soup for the Teacher's Soul: Stories to Open the Hearts and Rekindle the Spirits of Educators.* New York: Health Communications.

Intrator, Samuel M., and Parker J. Palmer. 2002. *Stories of the Courage to Teach: Honoring the Teacher's Heart.* New York: John Wiley and Sons.

Jennings, Kevin, ed. 1994. *One Teacher in Ten: Gay and Lesbian Educators Tell Their Stories.* Los Angeles: Alyson Publications.

Logan, Judy, and Peggy McIntosh. 1999. *Teaching Stories.* Tokyo: Kodansha Press.

Ohanian, Susan. 1995. *Ask Ms. Class.* Portland, ME: Stenhouse.

Mentoring Through Goal Setting: "Where Are We Going and How Do We Know We Have Arrived?"

One aspect of mentoring is helping beginning teachers establish appropriate, reachable goals. Just as teaching is often described as a journey, goal setting can be the road map to professional development. By making specific goals, beginning teachers can understand the intended destination and chart a course to arrive there.

During a conference before or early in the school year, mentors and mentees can discuss appropriate, basic, and concrete goals. Unrealistic goals for a first-year teacher might include writing a computer lab grant or helping the school move to student-led parent-teacher conferences. Although each of those goals has merit, each one may be too ambitious for first-year teachers. First-year teachers may need to focus on such basics as curriculum development, classroom management, and organization. This chapter describes six ways that mentors and beginning teachers can determine appropriate goals:

1. assessing strengths and weaknesses

2. building teacher confidence

3. analyzing teacher preparation and classroom management

4. evaluating active learning practices

5. supporting professional development

6. analyzing teacher standards

After determining ways to form effective goals, we will examine ways to assess progress toward attaining them.

Assessing Strengths and Weaknesses

Sometimes the mentor can ask the beginning teacher about teaching strengths and weaknesses and the two can form effective goals together. In the example below, Philip and Marcos, a first-year teacher, determine appropriate beginning teacher goals:

Philip: Are you ready to get the school year under way, Marcos?

Marcos: Sure, I'm psyched!

Philip: I remember from your interview that you have many teaching talents. Let's take a minute and you can jot some down.

Marcos: OK. Well, I like this age group.

Philip: That's a good trait to lead the list. What else?

Marcos: I like my subject area, and I like to think of creative ways of getting kids to enjoy math.

Philip: Creativity, that's good.

Marcos: I like to show how math is used in our daily life. Instead of just learning about percents, I like to show students how they can use percents. For instance, during student teaching I showed the top ten hit songs and asked students to figure out the percent of male and female lead singers.

Philip: Great idea. The kids probably loved that.

Marcos: (smiles) Uh-huh, they did. I also like to have the students do projects.

Philip: Sounds good. What kind of projects?

Marcos: Well, they had to figure out how to measure for perimeter, area, and volume, so I brought in Styrofoam blocks and let the kids experiment with a variety of shapes like squares, rectangles, and pyramids.

Philip: So you like to use active learning in your teaching?

Marcos: Yeah.

Philip: OK, in the plus column are liking middle school students, enjoying math, being creative, and using active learning. How about the areas you'd like to work on? Be honest, now.

Marcos: Well, I think I need to work on organization.

Philip: (laughs) Me, too! How would you like to be more organized?

Marcos: I can always come up with good ideas, but I'm worried that I won't be able to keep the continuity within the unit. During my student teaching, I could bounce things off Chris.

Philip: Would it be helpful if we sat down on Friday and talked through the coming week?

Marcos: Really? If you have the time, that would help me feel more confident about what I'm doing.

Philip: OK, I wrote down "conferences to focus on unit planning." At least we can try that for the first few weeks to get you going.

In this scenario, Philip leads the conference by questioning Marcos about his positive traits, an effective way to help a beginning teacher gain confidence. Then by asking about weaknesses, Philip guides Marcos toward tackling a goal such as organization. By using this approach, Philip gives ownership to Marcos, causing him to determine and be more responsible for his goal. If Philip had begun the conference by saying that most beginning teachers lack organization, Marcos might have felt defensive. Because Marcos initiates this goal, the two can work together more collaboratively.

If beginning teachers have difficulty defining specific goals, mentors might suggest teacher confidence, lesson preparation, classroom management, and/or student assessment as effective starting points.

Building Teacher Confidence

Although Marcos seemed self-confident about certain areas such as his creativity, many beginning teachers feel less self-assured. In the following example Maribeth tries to help Perry, her student teacher, set a second type of goal, increasing his self-confidence:

Maribeth: We've now had a couple of weeks of school. Shall we set some goals for the semester?

Perry: Sure.

Maribeth: What would you like those goals to be?

Perry: Everything—getting to know the students, using good classroom management, preparing my lesson plans, using technology, working with parents. (laughs) I think I need help with everything.

Maribeth: It probably does seem overwhelming now, but we can take it one step at a time.

Perry: OK, but I need to learn everything.

Maribeth: You have many good teaching traits. You've been here only a couple of weeks and you know most of the students' names, you've responded to students' papers, and you've working with students one-on-one and in small groups.

Perry: Yeah, but I have a lot to learn.

Maribeth: Well, that's a good attitude. Maybe we should work on your confidence.

Perry: (laughs) Uh-huh. I need that, too.

Maribeth: How do you think we can increase it?

This exchange indicates that Perry first needs to recognize strengths and then focus realistically on a few goals. Maribeth wisely suggests that they may need to discover ways Perry can explore his own strengths and that building confidence can itself be a goal.

Students quickly notice a beginning teacher's lack of confidence. Mature students may be empathetic, but immature students may take advantage of the situation. Beginning teachers who are unsure of their own knowledge or effective procedures may inadvertently lower expectations, extend deadlines, or reduce assignments. Often mentors need to show beginning teachers how to adopt an air of confidence. When the beginning teacher appears confident, students usually reciprocate by following the teacher's leadership. This, in turn, increases the beginning teacher's actual self-confidence or self-efficacy. Although appearing self-confident might seem to be a short-term bridge, a self-assured attitude carries long-term implications.

Often mentors must help beginning teachers through their emotions before targeting intellectual and academic issues. The following interaction shows Maribeth's direct approach to helping Perry:

Perry: I guess if I have some good class periods, I'll start feeling more confident.

Maribeth: That's true, but we can't wait that long. If you're scared or nervous, the students will sense it.

Perry: But I am really nervous. How do I not show that?

Maribeth: If you're really prepared, know exactly what activities you're going to do, and have the materials all laid out, you're more likely to feel confident.

Perry: OK.

Maribeth: Standing erect and speaking with a strong voice also give impressions of being confident.

Perry: So I'm supposed to fake it?

Maribeth: Well, that's one way of looking at it. Teachers must often be actors.

Perry: (laughs) OK. Is there anything else I can do?

Maribeth: I've found that it helps to "dress the part." When I look like a teacher, I'm more apt to act like a teacher. I encourage you to do the same.

Perry: I never thought of it that way. I just thought I should dress like the kids so they'll like me.

Maribeth: It's natural to want to be liked, but do you think it's more important to be liked or for students to be learning?

Perry: Yeah, I guess you're right. Not only will I be super prepared, but I'll try the tie bit. My college professor said that was a sure winner.

Maribeth: Remember that the first person you need to convince is yourself. (Both laugh.)

Although Maribeth and Perry conclude the conference on a light note, most mentors recognize that helping beginning teachers gain confidence sometimes requires infinite patience. Maribeth provides concrete examples of ways to improve confidence. Perry can take outward steps to help himself feel more professional; these steps may lead to others' laudatory comments and/or his own positive internal feelings, increase his teacher pride, and develop his self-confidence. Other strategies are for mentors and beginning teachers to plan and teach together so the novice teacher can feel assured that the first teaching instances are not "do or die." Looking for and commenting on positive teacher growth also helps further the process. For some novice teachers, gaining confidence is a semester-long or year-long endeavor.

Analyzing Teacher Preparation and Classroom Management

In addition to assessing strengths and weaknesses and building teacher self-confidence, a third method of goal setting is to analyze the most problematic areas for beginning instructors: teacher preparation and classroom management. Many new teachers may experience problems before they fully understand that the two may be interconnected: poor planning often leads to classroom management difficulties. Often student teachers form the misimpression that experienced educators, who seem to teach so easily and naturally, are doing so with little or no preparation. Whether because of overconfidence, lack of time, or emotional stress, beginning teachers often experience planning problems. Note in the following scenario how a mentor can use questioning to initiate a goal-setting plan:

Nate's student teaching experience started well. He and Rosalee, his mentor, planned and taught the first unit together. Then Nate attempted to teach bar graphing to fifth graders. After he modeled the lesson, the students created and shared their own graphs. However, after this activity, fifteen minutes remained. He rushed to the back of the room. "What should I do, Rosalee? I'm finished with everything I had prepared."

Rosalee advised, "Why don't you take a poll of the students' eye colors and make a bar graph on an overhead transparency?"

"Great! Thanks, Rosalee," Nate said, hurrying back to the front of the room.

During their conference afterward, Rosalee questioned Nate about the instance, and Nate said he had learned the benefits of overplanning.

A few days later, a similar situation occurred. This time Rosalee decided not to be the rescuer. When Nate appeared at her side, she said, "It's your class, Nate. What are *you* going to do?" She smiled reassuringly. "I'm sure you can manage."

She moved to the back of the room and watched, ready to jump in if needed while inwardly hoping that Nate could successfully resolve the situation. She watched as he put students into groups of four and had them create a bar graph of their number of siblings. Suddenly hands shot up all over the room. "Should I count my stepsister, Mr. O'Brien?" "What about my brother who is away at college?" "I have two sisters who are married. Do I count them?" "My mom is expecting. Can I count the new baby?" Nate responded to each student's question with a quick answer, and as the bell rang, he sighed noticeably.

After school, Rosalee asked, "How do you think today went?"

Nate shook his head. "Well, I thought I was prepared, but once again, I hadn't prepared enough. Then I gave them an assignment I hadn't really thought through, and I wasn't ready for all of their questions."

Rosalee smiled and nodded. "I liked how you were able to respond with an assignment and answer their questions. The important question, though, is what can you do to prevent this problem?"

Nate pointed to his plan book. "From now on, I'm going to overplan each lesson and consider all the details."

As shown by Rosalee's mentoring approach, mentors often walk a fine line between rescuing and letting beginning teachers struggle, and between offering direct versus indirect coaching. Mentoring often involves a balancing act of deciding when to approach a problem head-on and when to use questioning to let the beginning teachers make discoveries. Rosalee uses a scaffolding method of rescuing Nate the first time (to build his confidence) and then allows him to flounder and improvise the second time (to increase his independence). Similarly, during the first conference, she asks Nate directly about the problem, but in the second instance she uses the open-ended question "How do you think today went?"

As an effective mentor, Rosalee realizes that the most common error for beginning teachers is the lack of careful planning. Sometimes teachers think they are prepared but don't realize the full level of readiness required. For instance, a beginning teacher may think he or she thoroughly understands the preamble of the Constitution but finds it difficult to convert large democratic principles into common student vocabulary. Later, the beginning teacher may say, "I practiced in my head. It just didn't come out right when I spoke." For particularly difficult concepts, the mentor may suggest practicing aloud before a mirror, to a group of family members or friends, or to the mentor herself. Beginning teachers also should realize that large concepts sometimes require several teaching days or that the concept may need to be broken into smaller segments. Mentors might pose one of the following questions to the beginning teacher:

- "What example are you going to use to explain the concept?"

- "What is another example you can use if some of the students still don't understand?"

- "What if the students request more examples?"

Experienced teachers may be adept at thinking on their feet, but beginning teachers may fare better by devising several examples before teaching.

The following scenario illustrates another common beginning teacher dilemma—inadequately preparing for early finishers:

Sam watched as Jennifer, his student teacher, administered a science test. As students turned in their papers, Jennifer sat at her desk and began checking them, oblivious to the rest of the classroom. Several students asked if they could go to the bathroom or get drinks, and she absentmindedly nodded her head.

Sam walked toward her and whispered, "Do you realize that the students are off task?"

Surprised, Jennifer looked up. She noted that several students were milling around the room, sharpening pencils, throwing away papers, and talking to each other. In her teacher voice, she announced, "If you're finished with your test, then get busy on some of your other work."

Hands waved in the air. "But I don't have any other work, Ms. Baker." "May I go to my locker?" "Could I go to the library?"

Jennifer looked at Sam, who gestured with his hand that she was in charge. "Either work on one of your other assignments or read a book. If you don't have a book, you may get one from our class library." Ten bodies started toward the classroom shelves. "And only two people at the bookshelves at a time. While you're waiting, sit quietly."

During their prep period, Jennifer reflected, "I spent all week working on making a good test, but I didn't think about the chaos that could occur if some students finish the test earlier than others. I guess I should have had another activity or told them earlier in the day to bring their free-reading books."

Sam smiled. "I'm glad that you're noticing what makes a well-run classroom."

Jennifer's neglect of early finishers is a common beginning teacher problem. Most beginning teachers do not consider this predicament until they assign small-group work and one group finishes quickly while other groups may just be getting started. Before the class period, mentors might ask, "How have you planned for early finishers?" After preparing beginning teachers for this likely event, mentors can usually wait until the situation arises. In this instance, Sam decides to alert Jennifer to the problem but to allow her to resolve it. If and when the situation reoccurs, beginning teachers can usually self-correct and rediscover the importance of preparing for early finishers.

However, even after the beginning teacher fully comprehends the scope of preparation needed, the failure to fully prepare sometimes resurfaces. After a series of successful lessons and increased confidence, sometimes the beginning teacher, such as Joel in the following instance, decides to circumvent the process:

After a weekend in his hometown, Joel arrived in his classroom unprepared for the lesson on fractions. Telling himself, "Oh, I'll just wing it," he found that he hadn't thought through how to explain changing the denominator or reducing fractions.

Later, he admitted to his mentor, Suzanne, "Well, I did it again. Things have been going so smoothly, but today I fell flat on my face. I had too good a time this weekend—so good I wasn't prepared for today. The kids were getting frustrated and loud. Even though I got mad at them, the person I should have gotten mad at was me."

Suzanne nodded. "I've found that lack of preparation often leads to classroom management problems."

"Uh-huh. When I'm prepared, I feel more confident. I know what I'm going to do, I'm ready with more examples if I need them, and I know how to switch directions if the students sail through the lesson. If I know what steps to take, the kids seem to follow along and participate rather than acting up. Nothing beats preparation!"

As Nate, Jennifer, and Joel learn the importance of overplanning, preparing for early finishers, and not "winging" it, they realize that effective preparation often eliminates other classroom problems. Mentors usually need to coach beginning teachers, at first directly and then indirectly, to help them recognize the importance of planning. They must decide when to rescue, when to ask questions about teacher preparation, and when to allow beginning teachers to stumble and come to their own realizations.

Because most novice teachers struggle with planning, mentors can help them make it one of their key goals. Another common problem for beginners is classroom management. Most teacher education programs include classroom management strategies, but classroom management practices usually depend on the specific situation. Although many beginning teachers can espouse their classroom management philosophies, enacting these beliefs may depend on the students, the school environment, or the particular incident. (See Chapter 5 in *Mentoring Beginning Teachers* for more examples of ways mentors can assist with classroom management challenges.)

Evaluating Active Learning Practices

A fourth type of goal-setting strategy involves evaluating active learning practices. In the following vignette, Keesha and Camilla discuss group and individual teaching techniques:

As an artist, Keesha had worked with oils, watercolors, fabrics, and pottery, so she felt at home in the art classroom. As a forty-year-old provisionally licensed teacher, though, she was learning for the first time how to work with students. She discovered that an eighth-grade class offered special challenges.

"They don't listen to me," Keesha complained to her mentor, Camilla, another art teacher in the building. "I give a lecture on shadows, and they're looking around the room, not even paying attention."

Camilla laughed. "That sounds like eighth graders. They like to be active. Have you tried using light to create shadows and then asking students what they observe?"

"No, that sounds like too much work. Why should I do that when I can just tell them what happens?"

"I've found that students learn more when they discover things for themselves. When students construct their own knowledge, it seems to sink in more."

"OK, I guess I could try a new lesson on shadows. Another problem, though, is that when I walk around the room and tell students what they can do to improve their drawings, they get mad at me. They can't take constructive criticism. When I take their pencil and show them how it's supposed to look, they seem to resent me."

Camilla nodded. "I've discovered the same thing. Instead of telling them what is wrong, I start by telling them what is right or that they've chosen a good subject. Then I start asking questions. For instance, right now I'm trying to teach perspective, so I've been having students draw objects such as tables, sidewalks, or buildings. Many of them can't understand that a table's front legs should be drawn longer than the back legs. I've been using all kinds of visuals such as films that I put on pause or overhead transparencies of objects. I've even used the real estate pages to show how the windows at the back of a house are smaller than the front windows. Then I ask questions about the size of objects compared with the distance. When they can see it, they usually get it."

Keesha responded, "OK, I guess I can do that. But can't I still correct their drawings?"

"You know, when I change the student's work, the student just thinks, 'I didn't do it right. I can't do it.' However, when I ask questions and show examples, the students usually can make the changes themselves. Then they've learned something and they feel good about what they've created."

"OK. That's not how my teachers taught me, but I guess I'll give it a shot."

Although many teacher education programs emphasize active student learning, sometimes called a constructivist philosophy, beginning teachers, especially older, nontraditional ones who have not experienced this type of learning, often resort to the familiar technique of lecturing. Mentors can assist beginning teachers with this philosophy by discussing it in mentoring conferences or modeling it. Instead of being told how to change their pedagogy, novice teachers are most often influenced by observing successful teaching. When Camilla provides specific examples of how she uses demonstrations such as light and shadows, visuals such as films or overhead transparencies, or questioning to evoke student thought, she shows rather than tells Keesha what works for her in the classroom. Mentors can encourage beginning teachers to make an active learning approach one of their goals.

Supporting Professional Development

Some mentor–beginning teacher teams may wish to use some of the aforementioned practices for goal setting, whereas others may examine methods of supporting professional development. Effective first-year teachers or teachers in their second or third year of teaching may wish to challenge themselves further. Delores Westerman (1999) lists four qualities of experienced teachers:

Integrated Learning   Experienced teachers integrate and draw connections between current, past, and future learning, and other content areas. Beginning teachers tend to rely solely on grade-level curriculum objectives or benchmarks and have more difficulty making cross-disciplinary connections. They usually do not have the time or vision to investigate the curriculum of other grade levels or disciplines.

Classroom Management   Veteran teachers possess and use a repertoire of classroom management techniques such as voice, gestures, proximity, and reading students' body language. On the other hand, beginning teachers often ignore off-task behavior until it escalates, and then interrupt the lesson with a verbal reprimand or punishment. Experienced teachers are more likely to use preventive strategies, whereas beginning teachers wait for the problem to arise and then react.

Whole Picture   Experienced teachers are more likely to see the "big picture." In planning lessons, they visualize the lesson, predict problems, and prepare alternative activities. Novice teachers, however, tend to "try it to see if it works." Instead of anticipating how certain activities will play out in the classroom, they often wait for problems to arise.

Needs Assessment Experienced teachers know their students' needs and evaluate their lessons according to students' learning growth. Beginning teachers, on the other hand, often judge their lessons according to students' positive or negative reactions. They evaluate whether the students have met the original objective but usually don't place it in the context of students' needs.

Together the mentor and beginning teacher may determine which of the four experienced-teacher qualities are the beginning teacher's strengths and which one or two areas could be professional-development goals. In the following conversation, Marian and Deena, a second-year teacher, discuss Deena's future goals, framed by Westerman's list of teacher qualities:

Marian: In looking over Westerman's four areas, which ones do you think are your strengths?

Deena: I think I'm best at needs assessment. When students walk in the room, I remind myself of the objectives I need to accomplish. Then when the bell rings and the students walk out the door, I ask myself whether they have learned that specific objective. During student teaching, I used to evaluate the lesson according to whether the students seemed to be paying attention and having fun, but now I look for whether learning has occurred. I also evaluate the lesson according to the state standards and district benchmarks.

Marian: Great! You sound like a master teacher!

Deena: Not really. Sometimes another class comes in, and I don't have time to reflect on what has happened, but I try to find time at the end of the day.

Marian: That's good. So which of these areas do you see as a weakness or one you would like to work on?

Deena: I think I'll start with the first one, integrated learning. I've been concentrating on the state standards for social studies in fourth grade, so I understand pretty well what's happening at my grade level. I just have a general idea, though, about what is being taught at third grade and what is expected at fifth grade. Since I teach only social studies, I also don't know what other units are being taught in fourth-grade reading, language arts, math, and science. I meet with my team, but we usually talk about specific students or plan our end-of-the-year interdisciplinary unit. We haven't had time to talk about our own units during the year. I know I should help students make connections to previous and future learning as well as to their interdisciplinary work.

Marian: It sounds like you want to do both vertical articulation of grade levels and horizontal articulation across disciplines in fourth grade. That's a terrific goal, but it sounds rather large. How could you narrow it down?

Deena: You're right. I think that this year I'll work on just learning about what happens in third-grade and fifth-grade social studies, what you called vertical articulation. Then I can understand better what prior knowledge students have, and I can see how this will scaffold into fifth grade. I can wait until next year to work on adding more interdisciplinary units.

Marian: That's a good plan.

By concentrating on one objective at a time, beginning teachers are more likely to accomplish a specific goal. Rather than Marian telling Deena her own opinion about Deena's strengths and weaknesses, she leads Deena through a self-reflective session and lets her devise her goals. She focuses first on Deena's strengths and then questions and paraphrases Deena's goals. When Deena attempts too much—both vertical and horizontal articulation—Marian gently steers her toward one goal at a time, but again allows her to decide the specific goal. Deena's decision to examine the objectives or benchmarks at the previous and later grade levels will allow her to obtain a bigger picture of where students have been and where they are going. She can now review past knowledge and make connections to future curricular objectives, helping her feel more confident about enabling and enhancing student learning. While Deena makes the decisions for her own goals, Marian guides her through the process. By using Westerman's teacher qualities as a guide, she is assured that Deena will select a worthwhile goal; by encouraging a narrow focus, she helps Deena determine an attainable goal. If Marian were to carry the process to another level, she might even decide upon her own goal for professional development, so she could model lifelong teacher growth.

Analyzing Teacher Standards

A final goal-setting option for early-career teachers is to examine state or national teacher standards. Most states have created their own teacher standards, as have the National Council for Accreditation of Teacher Education and the Teacher Education Accreditation Council. By perusing these standards, the mentor and beginning teacher can decide which ones to target as goals.

For instance, if the mentoring pair decide upon a goal of improving assessment, they might discuss specific areas such as developing a plan for late or makeup work, responding to written papers, using the district computer-grading program, creating rubrics or alternative assessments, accommodating special-needs students and second-language learners, or planning for parent-teacher conferences. Mentoring conferences that focus on district expectations, benchmark levels of competency, alignment of assessment to standards, and meeting the needs of all students can be especially helpful.

Together the beginning teacher and mentor can analyze the teacher standards and determine effective goals. In the following dialogue, Julianne and Tanya discuss the teacher standard of improving parental communications:

Julianne: Let's look over these state teacher standards. Our principal will evaluate you on all of these, but she advised the mentors to have the beginning teachers decide upon one or two to work on specifically this year. Does that sound OK to you?

Tanya: Sure.

Julianne: Which one do you think you want to try?

Tanya: As a kindergarten teacher, I think I want to work on the one about relationships with parents and community.

Julianne: Great! What ideas do you have?

Tanya: Well, I plan to send a letter in August and then meet with parents during the open house before school. Most kindergarten teachers write a weekly note telling what's happening in the classroom and how parents can reinforce the learning at home. Maybe I can even do that twice a week.

Julianne: That would be nice, but be careful not to overcommit yourself. Planning for the next day comes before sending more letters home.

Tanya: OK, well, I've also heard of schools that have a Family Writing Night. I'd like the kindergartners to draw a picture, tell their parents a story about the picture, and have their parents write it for them or even type it on the computer. Later in the year, some of them will be writing words or phrases.

Julianne: Super! What are some of the advantages to that?

Tanya: Well, maybe the parents would even see this as a model and continue with the story-writing activities at home.

Julianne: Great!

Tanya: I'd also like to write notes about individual students to parents. I could send either e-mails or handwritten notes.

Julianne: I like your enthusiasm. As a P.E. teacher, I always thought all of this parent stuff was for the birds, but this summer a P.E. teacher from Mount Fraser told me she chooses two students each class period. She watches those two students that period and jots down notes about physical skills such as "catches ball easily" or social skills such as "takes turns well" or "is a good team player." Then while the kids are dressing or lining up, she writes a positive two-sentence note to the parents.

Tanya: What a good idea!

Julianne: If I see five P.E. classes in one day, I have an opportunity to write ten notes a day, which adds up to fifty notes a week. It sounds like a quick and easy way to communicate with parents. I think I'll try it for a few weeks and see how it goes.

Tanya: Good for you.

Julianne: I thought we were supposed to be coming up with ideas for you, but (laughs) now I have a parent goal, too. I guess we can both work on parent communication as our teacher-standard goal.

In this scenario, Julianne uses effective mentoring strategies to help Tanya arrive at an attainable goal. She gives Tanya ownership of goal setting, questions her to narrow her goals, focuses on the practicality of time, provides praise, offers an example, and models balanced goal sharing by creating her own goal. Using the state or national teacher standards can be an effective framework for goal setting, especially if these standards are part of the teacher evaluation system. As we reiterate throughout this book, mentoring and evaluation should be separated, but it would be logical for the beginning teacher to select one of the teacher standards and work toward improvement in that area.

Assessing Beginning Teacher Goals

After the beginning teacher—with the mentor's guidance—has established one to three goals for the school year, the two teachers need to determine steps to achieve these goals and ways to assess progress. In some cases, the steps might have specific dates of attainment; in other cases, the process might be more integrated. Some goals, of course, are more adaptable to a step-by-step approach than others. For instance, it might be easier for Nate to determine whether his teacher preparation includes alternative ideas, extra examples, and work for early finishers than it would be for Perry to assess how much his teacher confidence is increasing. Similarly, Deena's goal of vertical articulation and Tanya's goal of parental communication may be ongoing goals rather than ones quickly attained. Whatever the situation, the mentor might ask, "How do you think we can determine when you have reached this goal? What are some steps you can take? What are some ways we can assess your progress?"

Goal assessment can become part of the weekly mentoring conference or it can be set aside for special times during the year, such as at the beginning of a new quarter. Ways to analyze goal achievement might include the mentor and beginning teacher using one or more of the following methods:

- Make separate analyses prior to the mentoring conference and then share findings.

- Create a plus-minus chart of instances of goal attainment/lack of attainment.

- Devise a time line of when goals are met and unmet.

- Describe classroom examples when the goal was met/unmet.

- Share an e-mail or journal entry about meeting goals.

- Analyze and reevaluate the steps for accomplishing the goal.

- Reassess how you will know when the goal is achieved.

Creating Mentor Goals

The six goal-setting techniques described in this chapter have focused on goals for the beginning teacher. However, effective mentors also create goals for their own teaching and mentoring. Just as beginning teachers shouldn't feel isolated, mentors need to establish communication by talking and sharing with other mentors. Let's listen as Daryl, a new mentor, and Marla, a second-year mentor, discuss their upcoming year as mentors, as well as their own mentoring goals:

Daryl: This mentoring workshop has been pretty helpful. They said we're supposed to help the beginning teacher form goals, which is OK by me. But then they said we need to come up with our own mentoring goals. So what will be your goals, Marla?

Marla: Well, my first goal is to meet at least once a week with the beginning teacher. Last year I tried doing that, but we often got sidetracked and sometimes didn't meet for several weeks. This year I'd like to keep a tighter rein on that.

Daryl: That's good. Anything else?

Marla: Yes. I'm going to work on my questioning skills. These workshop leaders keep telling us that we should be questioners and listeners instead of advice givers and problem solvers. It's hard, though. When a new teacher comes to me, the first thing I want to do is give advice and solve the problem. It's a lot harder to ask questions.

Daryl: That one will be hard for me, too. When I teach driver's ed, I ask questions in the classroom. Out on the road, though, sometimes I have to give direct instructions to the student drivers. I can't ask questions if I think the driver is going to back into another car! After the car is stopped and we're out of danger, I ask questions about the situation. I realize a beginning teacher isn't a beginning driver, so I'm going to have to stop myself from giving immediate advice and work on my questioning skills. I don't know if I'll have enough patience, though.

Marla: (laughs) Believe me, Daryl, anyone who teaches driver's ed already has a ton of patience.

Daryl: Let's see: your goals are to meet weekly and ask questions instead of giving outright advice. Is it OK for me to borrow those goals or is that cheating?

Marla: It would be great if we have the same goals, Daryl. That way we can keep each other on track. We can mentor each other.

Daryl: Works for me!

In this scenario, Marla and Daryl discuss the value of reciprocal sharing in meeting their own mentoring goals. In addition to their goals of meeting regularly and asking effective questions, mentors might consider other mentoring objectives such as effective listening, preventing the beginning teacher's social isolation (see Chapter 5), watching for signs of teacher burnout (see Chapter 8), or coaching toward self-mentoring (see Chapter 9). While reading this text, you might list possible mentoring goals for yourself.

Summary

As a road map, goal setting helps the beginning teacher and mentor determine their destination and assess their progress. Six possible types of goal setting are assessing strengths and weaknesses, building teacher confidence, analyzing teacher preparation and classroom management, evaluating active learning practices, supporting professional development, and analyzing teacher standards.

Once the beginning teacher and mentor have established their goals, they can decide upon ways to evaluate and reassess how well they are reaching their intended destination. To determine progress, the two can use numerous assessment devices such as time lines, charts, journals, oral reflections, or other means.

Of course, professional growth should be a lifetime goal, and mentors can be effective models of both goal setting and goal analysis. Together the mentor and beginning teacher can adopt the role of learner, and the ensuing mentoring relationship can lead to mutual growth.

One of the most important goals will be maintaining the mentoring relationship itself. The mentor can help the beginning teacher move from stages of dependence to independence and even interdependence with school team members. In the same way, the mentoring relationship can slowly evolve from mentor-mentee to collegial collaboration.

PART

II

Responding to Challenging Situations

Age and Gender

I am so nervous about who [they're] going to give me for a mentor teacher. I'm really hoping for someone older than me but not so much older that she won't be able to understand where I'm "coming from." And it has to be a woman; I can't imagine working with a guy.

Thalia, first-year teacher

For many beginning teachers, being assigned a mentor who is much older (or younger in certain situations) or of a different gender creates great consternation in their young professional hearts. Many assume there will be a generation gap in knowledge and attitudes, or that a man and a woman working together will never be simpatico.

As we noted in *Mentoring Beginning Teachers,* the factors that should be considered in forming mentoring partnerships are as follows. The mentor should

- have a minimum of three to five years of teaching experience,
- teach in the same content area or at the same grade level,
- have a classroom (physically) close to that of the beginning teacher,
- be significantly older (eight to fifteen years), and
- be aware of gender differences. (p. 11)

However, the ideal situation may not always be possible. When it isn't, both members of the mentoring team may need guidance to be more successful in their interactions with each other. This chapter focuses on

- colleagues too close in age or too inexperienced,
- colleagues too far apart in age,
- colleagues at different places in their career,
- gender misunderstandings,
- when one teacher is gay or lesbian,
- attraction between beginning and mentor teachers, and
- matriarchal or patriarchal problems.

We will also provide some approaches and principles that may help support both mentor and beginning teacher as they forge their mentoring relationship.

Colleagues Too Close in Age or Too Inexperienced

Jena was asked to take a student teacher when she was twenty-three and in her second year of teaching. Even though her principal listed a number of reasons why he thought she would be a great mentor, Jena was horrified, mainly because she considered herself too young, too inexperienced, and too busy. Besides teaching five classes and supervising a study hall, Jena was the speech coach at her school. When would she have the time to sit down with the student teacher and make sure she had her lessons ready, her papers graded, and her questions, which would be many, answered?

However, Shawna, Jena's student teacher, was ecstatic that her mentor was young, had graduated from the same university—indeed, had taken the same courses with the same professors—and would understand where she was coming from. Shawna later told Jena she had pressured the university supervisor to place her with someone who was not considered a traditional teacher. In many ways it was easier for the two women to talk about pedagogical options and teaching strategies because they used the same language—writing process, reader-response, literature circles. However, these positive aspects of the similarity in age and background were offset by problems that Jena needed to deal with to guarantee Shawna a solid teaching experience.

For example, although Jena worked hard to be professional in her dealings with Shawna, too often, the student teacher wanted a friend with whom to gossip, discuss recalcitrant boyfriends, and share weekend plans. When Jena insisted that

Shawna begin planning for the classes she would soon teach, Shawna demurred, insisting that it would be better to keep using Jena's "tried and true" plans. Unsure how to proceed, Jena allowed Shawna to mimic her teaching for almost three weeks, then was horrified when the university supervisor came to visit and chided her for not pushing Shawna to take over the class on her own.

At the end of the semester, Shawna thanked Jena for being such an inspiring teacher, but Jena, while acknowledging that she had done the best she knew how for Shawna, wondered how much more inspired her student teacher would have been with a more experienced mentor.

This situation is a classic case of administrators making poor decisions although probably with the best of intentions. Jena's principal saw her as a rising star in his district, and thought that giving her a student teacher would be a reward for the good work she had done thus far. Shawna's university supervisor, who had also been Jena's supervisor two years before, knew that Shawna probably wouldn't stay in the teaching field unless she was inspired to do so, and he saw in Jena someone who might promote that spark in Shawna.

Problems

For Jena, however, mentoring Shawna created a number of problems. First, she never felt equipped to deal with a student teacher, and although both did their best, there was no way Jena could provide the depth of mentoring that a beginning teacher must have to be successful. On a pragmatic level, Jena lacked the experience to provide Shawna with enough information, teaching strategies, and management approaches for the time when there would be no supervision or, possibly, mentoring.

Second, Jena felt unable to say no to her principal because of her untenured status. Although she had a number of qualms that she shared with him when he offered her a student teacher, she did not question his decision too much because she didn't want him to think she wasn't professional enough to handle the situation. Jena also didn't feel secure enough as a professional to question her university supervisor; because she saw him as a mentor, she knew instinctively that he wouldn't assign Shawna to her if he didn't think she could handle it. In truth, Jena was pleased to be asked, and she felt a certain amount of pride in accepting a student teacher.

Third, Shawna also lost out, although her awareness of what she failed to gain from the experience was not as clear to her as it was to Jena. Jena had had a wonderful student teaching experience with an experienced teacher who went on to be her assigned mentor during her first year of teaching when Jena was hired by the same district. Jena tried to emulate her mentor as much as possible in her interactions with Shawna, but she knew she didn't always offer enough possibilities to feel that Shawna was as prepared as she could be for classes of her own.

Opportunities for Learning

What do we learn from a situation like this? First and most important, this example reinforces that very young teachers should not be given the responsibility of providing the main professional framework for other, more inexperienced teachers. It simply puts too much pressure on young professionals like Jena unless the principal or some other administrator is willing to take an active co-mentoring role. This co-mentoring might allow Jena to focus on content issues while the principal and Shawna spend more time discussing management and curricular issues. Nevertheless, the approach should be considered only if there is no alternative but to give a first- through third-year teacher a beginning teacher to mentor.

Second, teachers should not feel forced into taking a student teacher if they honestly don't think they are ready for one. Most teachers will admit that the first time the principal asked them if they were interested in hosting a student teacher or mentoring a beginning teacher, they resisted because they were concerned about "knowing enough." However, most eventually accept the responsibility because they know they had taught long enough to handle the situation. As discussed in Chapter 1, it is imperative that administrators make good decisions based on their knowledge of their faculty both as good teachers and solid mentors.

Finally, when a pairing like this does occur, the mentor teacher must be honest with the beginning teacher about her own strengths and weaknesses even as she evaluates the beginning teacher's abilities. An experienced mentor also typically does this to share with the mentee some of her own beginning teacher issues that she had to work through. Jena was instinctively correct in working hard to keep the relationship professional, and her unwillingness to become better friends with Shawna was commendable; most experienced mentors accept this as a necessary aspect of mentoring. One thing Jena could have done more of, though, was to involve the principal, the university supervisor, and other experienced teachers in Shawna's preparation so that Shawna would have been exposed to a better variety of practices and approaches to successful teaching. It seems clear that the pair was left too much to themselves as they struggled to build a mentoring relationship.

Obviously, the above situation is not ideal; but when one like it arises, it is important that certain ground rules or expectations be set through discussions among the participants in the fieldwork and mentoring experience. When new teachers are given student teachers because no more veteran teachers are available, the principal should be included, serving as a mentor to the new "veteran" teacher.

First, if the beginning and mentor teachers are similar in age, it is important that the student teacher understand that the mentor is not there to be a friend but a colleague. This distinction is necessary if the mentor teacher is to have any real authority in the situation. After all, the mentor is the one responsible for the activities and formal aspects of classroom life—dealing with parents, curricular decisions, grading—and must be able to set and guarantee certain professional guidelines for the beginning teacher.

Second, the principal or the university supervisor should plan to interact with the mentor and beginning teacher on a regular basis; for the university supervisor, this will probably mean more or longer visits to the fieldwork site. Videotapes to use to analyze the beginning teacher at work that can be sent to the supervisor may also be necessary if the supervisor cannot physically go to the site on a regular basis.

We also have to deal with some hard facts here. The student teaching semester (or year, in some situations) and the first year of teaching are make-or-break situations for many young teachers. Considering the severe shortage of teachers in this country and the high number who leave after one to two years, the profession can't afford mentoring situations such as the one above. How do we encourage smart decisions about placement when faced with this type of situation?

First, as noted in Chapter 1, administrators must be clear about the strengths and weaknesses of their teachers. Regular conversations and conferences with all teachers should be encouraged so that principal and educator may work together on each teacher's professional growth; some of this conversation may actually include whether a teacher feels ready to take on the mentoring of a new colleague. Furthermore, administrators must understand that no matter how wonderful a first- or second-year teacher is, that young professional is probably not ready for the emotional responsibility of mentoring a beginning teacher. If this is a student teaching situation, the principal may simply have to turn down the university's request for placement. This is sometimes difficult for principals because they like to have student teachers in the building for a number of reasons. School districts are always looking for qualified people to serve as aides and volunteers, and a student teacher fits that bill and more. Principals, like teachers, see taking student teachers as a professional responsibility, a "giving back" to the profession. Finally, in light of the current shortage of teachers around the country, a student teacher who has worked out well often becomes a new hire. Nevertheless, the refusal of placements with teachers who aren't ready for the responsibility is in the best interest of all concerned.

This leads to a reminder to university supervisors and placement offices. Although most student teachers are happy to allow their advisers or the university placement personnel to make their placements for student teaching, some, for legitimate reasons, ask for special consideration because of personal, family, or financial issues. Universities should make reasonable attempts to find these alternative placements, but they also need to say no to student teachers when there is a concern about how effective the placement may be. In some cases, student teachers are placed at a distance from campus for financial reasons, and often, the resulting placement is with another younger professional in the field. However, if a university supervisor cannot easily come for student observations or if the placement ends up being one where two new and inexperienced teachers are trying to teach each other, the placement should be changed. Money issues are important, but we are talking about long-term teaching careers, and student teachers who have such unsatisfactory experiences may choose never to teach. Our profession cannot afford to lose potentially strong and devoted teachers because of student teaching experiences that didn't need to be negative.

Colleagues Too Far Apart in Age

A disparity in age has the potential to create as many problems in the mentoring relationship as similarity in age does. As we said earlier, a difference of eight to fifteen years is considered optimal. Although we all know teachers in their late 40's, 50's, and 60's who are great mentors, there is a greater tendency for the experience to be less successful for all concerned when there is a twenty-five to thirty-year difference between the mentor and the beginning teacher.

Isobel, a veteran teacher who had been at Mattler Junior High School when it opened in the mid-60's, was still going strong at sixty-one. Her reputation around the school was iron-clad. "No one messes with Mrs. Baltron," it was said, and that included fellow teachers as well as her principal. When new teachers wanted to know the history of Mattler, they were sent to Isobel. She was also proud of the fact that the parents, aunts, uncles, and older siblings of the majority of her students had been her students, too. Often, when they came to parent-teacher conference night, they noted to Isobel and among themselves that nothing in her class had changed over the years.

When the school implemented a formal mentoring program in early 2000, Isobel was not one of the teachers asked to become a mentor. When she questioned the principal, he told her that he thought she would probably be retiring soon, and that he wanted to create mentoring relationships that would be sustained for up to five years. Assuring him that she had no intention of retiring "anytime soon," Isobel eventually became a mentor to Kaitlin, an enthusiastic twenty-four-year-old who came from a family of teachers. Kaitlin welcomed Isobel's mentoring and invited the seasoned teacher to view her classroom teaching. Kaitlin led her seventh graders through an interactive geography lesson in the school's computer lab, then took them to the library where, in groups of four, they researched the various geographic areas they had been studying. All this would lead to presentations the following day from each "expert" group. When the two teachers met at the end of the day, Isobel told Kaitlin that her reliance on computers was incomprehensible and that the students in the library hadn't been terribly respectful of the QUIET sign posted above the door. Furthermore, she noted, how was Kaitlin going to make sure that the groups had accurate information before they presented it? Although a subdued Kaitlin agreed with Isobel's concerns about the presentation of information, she realized that Isobel's teaching did not follow the same progressive leanings she embraced.

A short time later, Isobel asked Kaitlin to view her teaching. Isobel began with a review of the names of the men who signed the Declaration of Independence, then put her students in pairs and asked them to complete a worksheet using their notes and their text as needed. The students worked quietly for twenty minutes as Isobel walked around the room, responding to questions as they were asked. Toward the end of the class period, the students talked through their answers, and Isobel finished by reminding them of their test the next day and encouraging them to study that night. However, instead of asking Kaitlin what she thought of the class, Isobel told Kaitlin why her class had worked better than Kaitlin's in terms of management and meeting specific measurable objectives.

Kaitlin quietly withdrew from the mentoring relationship. Although she was still cordial to Isobel, she did not invite the senior teacher to view her classroom again. When Isobel came to her door to comment on Kaitlin's lack of worksheets and homework, to note that Kaitlin's class was viewing a movie again, and to raise Kaitlin's awareness of how loud her classroom seemed to passersby, Kaitlin simply smiled, thanked Isobel for her interest, and turned back to her planning.

Problems

In this situation, age, complicated by the fact that these two teachers were at different places professionally, made this a difficult mentoring relationship. Although neither teacher has anything to apologize for in terms of how she works with her students, it is clear from the example that both are coming from different pedagogical schools of thought. Isobel was quite happy with her tried and tested approaches, and nothing would change her mind; longevity often creates its own dynasty, and in teaching through so many generations of students, Isobel felt entitled to certain attitudes. On the other hand, Kaitlin was not wrong in her approaches, nor should she need to apologize to Isobel for her instructional methods.

When Isobel was asked why she thought the mentoring relationship wasn't working well, she said beginning teachers "don't want to listen to us . . . they don't respect us or what we've done in our classrooms." Beginning teachers like Kaitlin have been known to lament that their seniors "don't know the current trends, and won't listen to me when I try to share some of what I've learned in my classes." Although both views can be accurate, it seems obvious in the case of Isobel and Kaitlin that both wanted the mentoring relationship to be positive. With some guidance as to how to talk to each other, they could have gained from each other in various aspects of their teaching life.

Opportunities for Learning

In this relationship, it is clear that both mentor and beginning teacher needed to spend more time in productive listening to each other. "Productive" in this case would have meant that before Kaitlin even invited Isobel in to observe, the two would have sat down together and talked about their educational background. They would also have discussed some of the pedagogical approaches each thought worked well for her, and maybe shared some activities or exercises that had worked well in the past. This type of conversation would allow each to ask questions in a relatively safe environment. It is important to note that this should not be set up as an interview of sorts for the benefit of the mentor; this should be a more informal situation where the colleagues feel as if they can chat.

Another important aspect of this dialogue might focus on a discussion of current trends or issues facing teachers in general, those working in a specific content area, or educators in the school district. Again, this should be considered fact finding as opposed to figuring out that "Kaitlin uses radical approaches that I just can't approve of" or "Isobel isn't even aware of how competency testing for kids should be influencing her methodology." If the beginning teacher and mentor find it difficult to talk about these issues themselves or think they need other insights, this meeting might be held with other teachers in the content area. Often, the opportunity to hear a number of different ideas or approaches to the issues facing teachers in a department or program may help everyone think through what is in the best interest of students and colleagues alike.

Those of us involved in teacher training must also be careful in how we talk about older veteran teachers. Too often, teachers like Isobel are held up to beginning teachers as examples of what not to become. The reality is that most veteran teachers are as knowledgeable about current trends as their younger counterparts. A large number of veteran K–12 teachers have participated in the National Writing Project, for example, whereas new teachers usually don't have an opportunity to participate until they have been at their school for a few years. Those who have previously attended are asked to share their expertise with their colleagues, and in many schools, these post-project inservices are the first time many beginning teachers have worked through the writing process.

Sometimes a lack of communication about a pedagogical choice can create misunderstanding. Josh, a student teacher, shared how frustrating it was that his mentor, Daryl, didn't understand the power of the writing portfolio. When Daryl, Josh, and the university supervisor, Jean, sat down a few days later to discuss an observation, and Jean commented on Josh's use of the portfolio with students, Daryl asked Jean to explain how portfolios were different from the writing folders he had been using for years. As the three talked, they realized that they were all talking about writing and revision in much the same manner, but had different names for the receptacles where the writing was housed. Once Josh and Daryl understood that they were coming from the same pedagogical starting point, the tension that had originated in planning decisions disappeared and the relationship became more amicable.

Pedagogical issues aside, there is still much the beginning teachers can and should learn from veteran teachers, but the success will hinge largely on how effectively the local administration supports the mentoring relationship. There is a fine line between forcing mentorship and encouraging it. Often, beginning teachers have legitimate concerns about other people being in their rooms while they are trying new approaches or activities. If the activity fails, will the observer be expected to report it to the principal or department chair? In some cases, the observer may not be aware of the pedagogical choice because it is new to the field and the observer hasn't been in a college classroom or to a conference for many years. In that case, how will the observer truly understand what the beginning teacher is trying? There is also the reality of teachers who like the independence their classroom life allows and do not want to be compelled to share.

Colleagues at Different Places in Their Career

We may also see problems arise when the members of the mentoring relationship are at different stages of their career. We saw some aspects of this in the relationship between Isobel and Kaitlin in terms of their pedagogical approaches, but it is important to note that they were both still excited and dedicated teachers. The situation we consider in this section focuses more on teachers who, because of where they are in their careers, have different levels of dedication to the profession, their own professionalism, and their students.

Sabrina looked at the clock. Six minutes until her mentor, Darlene, was scheduled to come in for their weekly mentor meeting. Sabrina wondered what or who Darlene would be complaining about today: the principal? the same troublemaker students in her class? the lack of respect from parents? When Sabrina had first been assigned to Darlene, she had been pleased that she would be working with a veteran teacher who seemed to be successful in her own classroom. But in that first meeting, Darlene had talked more about how many months she had until retirement—forty-seven—than she had about the positive features of Wellspring Elementary. And since their first meeting, it was obvious that Darlene cared less about mentoring her new colleague and more about complaining that "education and teaching have changed over the years." Sabrina had certainly heard an earful from Darlene about how the profession had been better thirty years earlier. She was also well versed in how students used to be polite and quiet and parents used to be thankful for all that teachers like Darlene did for their children. What Sabrina hadn't heard were any comments about her own teaching that might have helped make her a stronger teacher. And from comments her colleagues had made to her in brief moments in the hallway, Sabrina realized that she wasn't the only one who was hearing Darlene's complaints about the profession.

Problem

In this case, it is clear that these two educators are experiencing a large "enjoyment gap" in their professional lives. As a beginning teacher, Sabrina was full of enthusiasm for her job, yet her delight in her work and students was slowly being eroded by Darlene's insistent carping and lack of interest in her colleague's work. On the other hand, Darlene thought that being asked to mentor a beginning teacher was simply another way for the school system to get more work from her without paying for the additional effort. Darlene's resentment wasn't really against Sabrina; indeed, she spent a lot of their meeting time warning the younger teacher of ways to elude additional duties "dreamed up" by the principal. But Darlene certainly did not see being asked to mentor Sabrina or any other beginning teacher as a tribute to her dedication to the profession or her excellent teaching.

Opportunities for Learning

This example clearly addresses the problems that occur when someone who is not excited about being a mentor is forced to become one. For Darlene, a great deal of this reluctance is related to where she is in her career. After twenty-seven years in the same school, she has weathered a number of principals, colleagues, and unruly students, and feels she has paid her dues to the profession. Yet the same tolerance she has shown in dealing with her career kept her from telling her principal that she wouldn't be a mentor. However, when forced into the situation, Darlene makes the decision, consciously or not, to do no more than she wants to with Sabrina, and in this case, all that becomes is complaining.

Obviously, the best way to handle this situation is to keep it from occurring. This will take honesty on Darlene's part and on Sabrina's part when asked to evaluate the mentoring situation. Many formal mentoring programs ask for evaluations of the experience at the end of each semester or at the close of the school year. Darlene should be forthright about her ambivalence even as Sabrina should be clear about the detrimental aspects of Darlene's mentoring so that another first-year teacher will not have to weather Darlene's feelings about her chosen occupation.

Gender Misunderstandings

Generally same-gender mentor pairings work most effectively. In larger schools, making these pairings happen will probably not be a problem; however, in smaller schools and especially in some secondary settings, there may be only two people in the department, and principals may be more concerned with best practice than gender balance. There are issues that may occur because of gender pairings, and in this section we look particularly at situations where gender misunderstandings may affect the development of the mentoring relationship, where one of the educators is gay or lesbian and problems that may occur when there is romantic tension between mentor and beginning teacher.

Gender Conflicts and Sexist Language

Beth was an articulate, organized, highly motivated senior looking forward to her student teaching experience. Her content knowledge was thorough, her writing exceptional, her theoretical concepts sure. For her college courses, she always read more than she was asked to and had developed a philosophy of education that was progressive and pedagogically sound. Her professors considered her one of the stars of the program.

Wes, a twenty-seven-year veteran of the classroom, was a wonderful teacher and powerful leader in his high school. His strong writing program was held up by his principal as one to be admired and fostered; his students had won a number of awards and prizes for their work. His students found him energetic and approachable; his colleagues saw him as professional yet friendly. He had been a cooperating teacher on a number of occasions; in fact, the university education program noted that he was "one of our best mentors for young professionals."

Most people would have considered the combination of these two bright, articulate people ideal for a student teaching placement. Indeed, it began that way, as Beth and Wes met and began planning together during the summer preceding Beth's fieldwork experience. However, during week one, the camaraderie that had developed began to fade when Beth heard Wes tell a female student he "liked her outfit" and another, "You look cute with your hair like that." As Beth paid more attention to what he was saying to students, she noted that Wes was "patronizing to girls, talking to them about clothes and hair. He didn't talk to the boys about things like that; he talked to them about sports and other, less superficial things."

Beth called her university supervisor, Kim, every other evening about Wes's "inappropriate language and behavior." "Doesn't he realize how sexist he's being?" she said. Regardless of Kim's suggestions to discuss the issue with Wes, Beth was so focused on the three minutes Wes spent chatting with students before and after class that she was not paying much attention to what made him, according to other teachers and students, a good teacher.

Wes also noted that Beth had changed her attitude toward him. She wasn't as willing to sit down and chat about methodological decisions, and he thought she was defensive whenever he questioned her pedagogical choices. However, she was asking him a lot of questions about his approach to working with male students versus female students, and he didn't think she liked his responses. In fact, he was tired of defending himself against what he considered the constant barrage of her questions. When he called to discuss the situation with the supervisor, he sounded a bit embarrassed as he said, "These young women today . . . they're so full of their ideas and why their approach to students is better. And she keeps asking me to talk about my experiences; it's like she wants to hear the story of my teaching career when I just want to tell her why I teach something a certain way and why it works. It was a lot easier last year with a male student teacher. Actually, I've always had male student teachers; maybe I'm not making the right adjustments for Beth."

Problems and Opportunities for Learning

Shortly after both had discussed their concerns with Kim, she asked them to talk with each other about why Wes's remarks and Beth's questions were creating so much tension. Wes was genuinely shocked when Beth handed him a sheet of comments he had made to his female students and said that she found his remarks offensive to women in general. He countered that he thought he was simply forging a friendlier tone for his classroom by speaking to the girls of more "social" things before class started; Wes said it had never occurred to him that the young women in his class might consider him sexist. He added that he never made comments of that type during class because it would take away from what needed to be accomplished. He also told Beth that none of the girls had ever complained to him about his comments, which he found telling, considering they argued with him over suggestions on papers or remarks made on class presentations. Nevertheless, he assured Beth, he would attempt to be more careful about what he said, especially because he was concerned that some of his female students might feel awkward or be afraid to confront him about his remarks.

Beth was equally shocked when Wes told her that he sometimes found her difficult to work with. Considering Beth more "high-strung" than the men he had worked with previously, Wes admitted that he wasn't always sure how to offer advice or constructive criticism, especially because she seemed to take everything he said so personally. As they talked through two different incidents that Wes saw as illustrating his concerns, Beth tried to work through why she had responded so negatively or, in one case, with tears, when Wes's comments had been fairly mild. Both agreed that they needed to be more honest and up front with each other about their feelings and concerns, especially because they were both concerned that a strained relationship between the two of them could negatively affect their students.

The above situation obviously focused on issues of gender and language, and the dissimilarity in Beth and Wes's professional personalities were highlighted because of the differences in where they were in their careers. However, this did not preclude them from addressing the issues directly in order to salvage the student teaching experience as well as the professional relationship. Wes did work on being more sensitive about the language he used, and Beth focused her energies on her pedagogical choices rather than listening for Wes to say something wrong. During Kim's supervisory visits, they talked about the modifications both were making in their interactions with each other and with students. Although they did not become lifelong friends, they still speak warmly of each other and the benefits of the student teaching experience. Both overcame the gender gap to profit from the relationship professionally.

Communication Issues

Ginge was proud of the fact that she had been chosen as a mentor teacher to three beginning teachers over the previous six years. In each situation, she had warmly welcomed her mentee, set up opportunities for full-class observations of the new teacher, and devoted one to two hours after school each week to discuss with her new colleague what had worked and what had been a challenge during the day's lesson. Her mentees, all women twenty-five to thirty-five years old, responded warmly to Ginge's offers of support, and the four still met one Saturday morning a month to discuss teaching in particular and life in general.

Thus, Ginge was not surprised when her principal called her in early July and asked her to take on a new mentee. "Luke has just graduated from the university and has been hired to teach sixth grade and coach the middle school boys' basketball team. He looks good, but his student teaching was split between second and fourth grade, so I'm hoping you can help him with curriculum issues and adjusting management styles with older students."

"No problem," said Ginge, and she went to school that afternoon and began preparing Luke's welcome notebook and curriculum guide. Because her principal had given her a number at which Luke could be reached, Ginge called and left a friendly message asking Luke to call back at his earliest convenience so they could set up a time to meet. Then she waited.

Luke, meanwhile, was looking forward to his new job and welcomed the information that he would have a mentor at the grade level at which he would be teaching. When he listened to his answering machine messages in the middle of July after returning from a short trip, he noted Ginge's message and wrote himself a note to give her a call.

Three weeks later, Luke called Ginge and they arranged to meet at school. As they chatted at their first meeting, Ginge mentioned that Luke must have had a busy summer since he had just been able to return her phone call. Luke responded that it had actually been a restful summer. The two looked at each other. Then Ginge said, "Well, shall we take a look at the welcome notebook and the curriculum?"

"Actually," said Luke, "I was hoping to take a look at them tonight and then get back to you with questions."

"Oh."

"Unless you really want to take the time today. . . ." Luke's voice trailed off. "I was hoping to do a few things in my room while I was here today so I don't have to come back again until the new teacher inservice starts."

"So you don't want to meet again before school starts?" Ginge was in turmoil. Didn't he realize that he was lucky to have her right here to go through things with him?

"Well, no, unless you really think we need to." Good grief, thought Luke. It was like having his mother hanging over him.

"Well, yes, I really think we should. I don't think you realize how much work is entailed in getting ready for the start of the school year. . . . Have you ordered your supplies, dropped off your book orders, discussed with Mrs. Nietman, our secretary, how the Xeroxing and supply cabinet works?" He's completely clueless, Ginge thought as she tried to mask her disgust.

"OK. OK. We'll meet next Friday and I'll have my questions ready." Anything to get her off my back, Luke thought.

"Fine."

At their second meeting, Luke soon realized that Ginge's favorite phrase was "Let's talk about. . . ." Ginge understood quickly that Luke was not interested in her experiences as a first-year teacher, nor did he seem to care much about her anecdotes concerning the beginning teachers she had worked with previously.

As the first weeks of school flew by, Ginge and Luke continued to feel conflicted about the time they had to spend together. Luke realized that if he didn't tell Ginge that he had only twenty minutes to talk, she would take sixty, waxing on about her experiences with portfolio assessment or a student's background. Ginge became annoyed at what she considered Luke's terse, noninformative responses about his classes and school life in general.

Their discordant feelings about each other came to a head the day Ginge went in to observe Luke's classroom. The class itself went well, and Ginge was happy to be able to sit down with Luke at the end of the day and tell him so; however, she had noticed one issue she particularly wanted him to deal with to make his classroom management more solid.

"I was noticing that you have a few students who are off task on occasion, especially when you're standing in the front of the room and using the overhead. Let's talk about how you might address that in the future," said Ginge.

"I just need to tell them to cool it, Ginge. And I need to look up more from the writing. Anything else?" asked Luke.

"Well, there are a few other ways to handle the overhead situation. I thought I could share with you some things I've learned and then we could brainstorm some additional approaches." Ginge looked at Luke expectantly. "For example, when I know that—"

"Look, Ginge, I really appreciate that you were able to come in and observe me today, but I've got a whole stack of math papers to grade and then I've got to get to the conditioning room and work out with the guys who are going out for basketball."

"Luke, I told you I was coming to observe and then to chat afterward."

"Yes, I know, but I don't think we need to turn this into a marathon conversation, and that's what it will be if I let you go on."

"I've just been trying to be helpful. That's been my only intention all along. I'm certainly not trying to waste your or my time." With that said, Ginge left the room feeling hurt and resentful. As she noted later to her former mentee Clarisse, "I just don't understand why he wouldn't want to take advantage of all my years of teaching experience. He could learn so much. Apparently, he already knows it all . . . but between you and me, he certainly doesn't!"

Luke felt resentful, too, as he turned the key in the lock a short time later and made his way to the school weight room. He had always hated it when his mother or girlfriends had "guilted" him into feeling bad for wanting to have short chats with them rather than tell them in detail about his life, school, and friends. Why did that type of attitude have to invade his professional life, too?

Problems and Opportunities for Learning

Various gender studies (Belenky, Clinchy, Goldberger, Tarule 1986; Tannen 1990) indicate that men and women may create knowledge in different ways. Such a gender difference may appear during discussion, whether it occurs formally or informally. According to Tannen's theories, men prefer to problem solve or "report-talk" by diagnosing and resolving the problem, and women prefer to talk through each issue in detail and confirm their feelings through "rapport-talk." Men may view short, focused conferences as being concise but see lengthy conferences as rambling time wasters. On the other hand, women may perceive the quick-solution method as too brusque and prefer talking through various causes, angles, and alternatives.

In addition, words or phrasing can be interpreted differently by gender. According to Tannen, "When women try to initiate a freewheeling discussion by asking, 'What do you think?' men often think they are being asked to decide" (p. 27). A male teacher may adopt the role of advice giver or problem solver when a female colleague merely wishes to have her feelings or perceptions confirmed. Tannen refers to these conversations as "cross-cultural communication" (p. 42). To avoid these conversational barriers, mentors may ask, "How can I help you work through this situation?"

Some studies (e.g., Dyson and Genishi 1994) indicate that women tend to use storytelling as a means of identity more than men, and other studies (e.g., Britton, Burgess, Martin, McLeod, Rosen 1975) suggest that women tend to prefer narrative over informative formats. If both teachers are aware of these tendencies, then storytelling—perhaps brief storytelling—can be honored during their conference together.

In situations like Ginge and Luke's, both participants need to realize that they are using different styles in their interactions with each other and that for the sake of the current mentoring relationship as well as their future professional interactions, they need to overcome their discomfort with the other style. For Ginge and Luke, it meant challenging themselves to move away from their own comfort zones to accommodate the other; it also meant that each had to talk honestly about what bothered them about the other person's communication style. Ginge explained to Luke why she considered teacher stories important; Luke shared his need to problem solve quickly and efficiently and his sincere dislike of tangents. Eventually, Luke and Ginge found a balance between brevity and deep thinking, and storied experiences versus briefer idea exchanges. As they did this, their mentoring conferences, as well as the mentoring relationship, became stronger.

When One Teacher Is Gay or Lesbian

Marcy, a student teacher in English, couldn't get over how brave her mentor teacher, Liza, was. It was only six weeks into her student teaching experience, and Marcy had team-taught books she considered pretty controversial for high school students. Now they were getting ready to start a unit on tolerance beginning with gay and lesbian issues. The students, juniors in high school, had been assigned Chris Crutcher's "In the Time I Have Left," a story about teenaged Louie Banks and the twentysomething man he befriends who happens to be homosexual and dying of AIDS. As the two women worked on their lesson plan for the day, Marcy told Liza how much she admired her willingness to make her students aware of the tough issues in life that they would face.

Smiling, Liza agreed that it was important to get kids to think critically. "And I think it's necessary to teach tolerance issues, so it becomes a great combination."

"But you also never seem to worry about parents getting uptight about your curriculum. When will I feel that way?" Marcy asked with a mixture of humor and earnestness.

"I guess I've just developed a tough skin," Liza responded with a smile. "And maybe it's also because no one has ever gotten very uptight with me directly about the fact that I'm gay, so I guess I figure that if parents and colleagues can deal with that, they can deal with my curricular choices."

"You're gay?!"

"Yes. I guess I thought you knew. It didn't occur to me to tell you."

"It's not that it matters really," said Marcy. "Does everyone know? The kids?"

"Well, once in while I'll hear some whispering and to be honest, last year when we were doing the Crutcher story, a few of the kids made some general comments questioning my sexual orientation, but if they're aware, most of them don't say anything. Mr. Fritz [the principal] knows, as do some of my colleagues . . . And it's not like I flaunt my sexuality. I don't feel that my personal life should necessarily impinge on my teaching, and you know how careful I am to stay the neutral course when we're having class discussions." Liza looked carefully at Marcy. "Is this going to cause problems for you?"

"No, of course not!" responded Marcy. Marcy meant it. Yet over the next few days, she found herself being careful in her conversations with Liza. She listened more carefully than she ever had to the words coming from her mouth. She became so concerned about not saying anything that Liza or anyone else might construe as her being aware of Liza's homosexuality that every conversation with or related to Liza became a tense situation for her.

Problem

Obviously, there are a number of gay and lesbian teachers in our schools, yet many straight teachers may not be aware of them because they, like Liza, don't choose to make an issue out of their sexual orientation. Do gay and lesbian teachers or their administrators have any particular obligations concerning student teaching placements or mentoring pairings?

Opportunities for Learning

First of all, teachers may choose to make this a nonissue. In the scenario above, Liza chose to tell her student teacher after they had been working together for six weeks. The two women had already established a strong professional relationship and got along well personally, and that may have been the reason Liza decided to share or confirm her sexual orientation with Marcy. However, many teachers might have simply responded to Marcy's question without revealing anything, and we would not fault either response. Sexual orientation is a personal issue that does not have to affect one's professional obligations. School administrators and university placement offices are not obliged to use knowledge of sexual orientation, on the part of a potential mentor teacher or a beginning teacher, to make placements. The bottom line remains that the relationship developed by mentor and beginning teacher is to be a professional one, not a personal one.

Marcy may, indeed, grow from this experience once she gets over her initial self-consciousness. The majority of us in education actively promote diversity within the field, and certainly, gay and lesbian teachers need to be part of this diversity. Knowing that Liza, an extremely successful practitioner, is in the profession is actually important to Marcy's professional growth. Yet Marcy needs to share with Liza her initial discomfort, not with her mentor's gayness but with her own inability to normalize the situation for herself. Marcy's hyper-awareness of Liza as a lesbian is fairly typical for many as they experience friends and colleagues coming out to them, and an honest interchange between the two is necessary. In this case, Liza would be able to help Marcy over her word-choice consciousness with humorous asides or reassurances that she has not been offended by anything Marcy has said.

Liza also ran a potential risk in sharing with Marcy because Marcy might have been homophobic, or at the very least, uncomfortable enough for it to negatively affect not only her relationship with Liza but her interactions with students and administrators as well. Marcy might have insisted on being removed from the student teaching placement and being put in another; although not necessarily a negative recourse, it would not be the best choice for Marcy or any student teacher's professional progress. If Marcy's request were made publicly, it might bring attention to Liza and the school, resulting in potential problems for the teacher and her administrators as they respond to those in the community who might not be open-minded. This could affect Liza's success in the classroom unless she has developed such a strong connection with her students that they are not bothered by her sexual orientation.

We might see some of the same difficulties if the student teacher or beginning teacher were gay or lesbian and dealing with a straight mentor, and the potential repercussions could be equally disastrous for the new teacher. A veteran mentor might have a great deal of influence with administrators who might put additional obligations on the beginning teacher. In a more conservative town or city, the veteran might share this information with a friend who shares it with another, and pretty soon the new teacher's sexual orientation is a topic of conversation over coffee in the local cafes and restaurants.

Issues concerning curricular choices might also become problematic because of mentor/mentee differences. For example, Liza tells Marcy she wants students to consider tolerance as it applies to their lives; obviously, Liza is selecting stories and discussion topics that allow her students to respond to a variety of issues that affect everyone. But if Marcy were actually Liza's colleague and the two were asked to delineate a number of literary selections that would be used by all educators in the district who taught tenth-grade English, Marcy might think Liza had actually chosen the Crutcher short story to force their students to deal with homosexuality and homophobia. If Marcy were uncomfortable with this aspect of tolerance education and knew Liza was gay, Marcy might be unable or unwilling to question her mentor about the choice of the short story. On the other hand, Marcy might feel strongly that Liza was politicizing the school curriculum to further her own agenda. Although they might be able to talk through Marcy's concerns about Liza's choices, it is also possible that the two would be so mired in the "correctness" of their individual approaches to tolerance education that they might not be able to discuss the situation honestly, resulting in a rift in the relationship that might never be mended.

These possible negative responses are not offered to keep teachers comfortable with their sexual orientation from sharing that information with others if they so decide. Sexual identity shouldn't matter in the profession one way or the other. However, each mentoring relationship is different, and those involved are best able to discern how much information can or should be shared.

Attraction Between Beginning and Mentor Teachers

Derek and Mallory got along well. They laughed at each other's jokes, finished each other's sentences, and were known to spend a great deal of time outside of school together. They were both single, and Mallory had been assigned to be Derek's mentor when he had joined the staff at the high school. Both in their late 20's, Derek and Mallory quickly found they had more in common than science. For them, the mentoring opportunity, in which Mallory was expected to offer support without reporting on Derek's successes or failures to the principal, became the story their best man told at their wedding.

Attraction between teachers can and does occur. In Derek and Mallory's case, this attraction, which led to a permanent relationship, had little effect on their professional lives with the exception of their reaction to the jibes they received from their students when they began attending school events together. Even though they might have been able to become a voting bloc in science department actions—there were only three teachers in the whole department—the professional repercussions for them were practically invisible.

Of course, if all attractions were as straightforward as Derek and Mallory's, there would be no need for this section in the chapter. So let's take a look at two examples that illustrate the potential pitfalls of work romances, especially when the relationship occurs between people in different power positions.

Situation 1: Student Teacher Falls for Veteran Mentor

Harry was one of those charming men everyone liked; in addition, he was considered a popular and successful teacher by all who knew him. A favorite of the university placement personnel, Harry could be counted on to take student teachers at the last minute. His principal called him the "miracle mentor" because everyone he worked with felt more comfortable and sure of him- or herself after listening to his motivational words. When Jordana was assigned to Harry as his new student teacher, no one was surprised when they hit it off, with the possible exception of Jordana, who had been extremely nervous about being placed with a male mentor.

As the weeks passed, Jordana found herself spending every moment she could with Harry and actually resenting the times she had to teach the class by herself so that Harry could absent himself from the room. Midway through the semester, Jordana invited Harry out for supper at a local restaurant; he accepted, and midway through the evening, she told him that she cared for him. A flustered Harry excused himself from the dinner, and the next few days at school were tense as he attempted to ignore and physically separate himself from his student teacher at every occasion. Jordana apologized on a number of occasions and tried to convince Harry that she could keep her feelings to herself, but the camaraderie built during the first half of the semester was gone.

Harry called the university supervisor, demanding that Jordana be removed from his classroom and placed elsewhere. He admitted that he was nervous in Jordana's presence. He also asked for assurances from the supervisor that she would handle the situation quickly and quietly, because he was concerned that Jordana might retaliate by accusing him of sexual harassment.

Upset that Harry wanted her out, Jordana questioned what her sudden disappearance from what had been a successful student teaching placement would mean to her future job goals. She wanted the supervisor to make Harry keep her on in the classroom and promised to say nothing to Harry about her crush on him, a crush that had ended abruptly when Harry indicated that he did not return those feelings.

Problems

Besides reminding us of the mantra of "same-gender pairings," this situation provides a clear example of why professionalism should be maintained between colleagues. Ideally, Harry and Jordana would have sat down together, discussed their mutual embarrassments, and agreed to continue on in a professional manner. However, Harry thought Jordana had compromised their professional relationship and did not see any way to handle it except to have her removed from the professional picture. Striving to be professional, he nonetheless felt "caught" because he suspected people would think that he, an older man, might have put pressure on Jordana to enter into a romantic or sexual relationship. He was also concerned that the jilted beginning teacher might attempt to hurt him personally and professionally. With these thoughts in mind, Harry wasn't able to articulate effectively to Jordana why he was now uncomfortable as the object of her affection, nor could he make himself believe her when she said that her feelings for him were gone.

Jordana, though, also had reason to be concerned about Harry's request to have her removed from the classroom. Because she was still doing her job well, and because she felt she truly was over her infatuation, she saw no reason why she shouldn't stay. Once Harry had said he wasn't interested, she had backed off and not mentioned the situation again, except to assure him that she would not bother him about it again.

Situation 2: Veteran Teacher Falls for Beginning Teacher

Marta, a beginning teacher in the district, was assigned to Robert for mentorship. As chair of the math department, Robert took seriously his duties connected to the hiring of new teachers and maintaining the quality of the courses delivered by the faculty in the department. This also meant that he observed the new teachers during their first three years in the department and was in charge of any remediation deemed necessary for those teachers—both beginning and veteran—who were having problems.

Marta and Robert got along well from the beginning, moving naturally from a strong professional relationship to a good personal association. Then, one weekend when they were writing a proposal for an Eisenhower grant, Robert told Marta that he was developing a romantic attachment to her. Marta told Robert that although she was honored that he saw in her someone he could be interested in, she had been dating a man she had known in college and they were getting pretty serious. Embarrassed, Robert tried to "backtrack," telling Marta that what he had actually meant was that he could be interested in someone like her. When they parted a short time later, Marta told Robert that he shouldn't be embarrassed and that she wouldn't tell anyone what he had said.

Within the next few weeks, however, Marta noticed that Robert had definitely cooled toward her. He rarely sat with her at lunch and avoided her as much as he could. When Robert came to observe her teaching, he seemed a great deal more critical about it than he had been in the past. Shortly afterward, they disagreed on a management approach she had taken with a student in the class. Instead of offering Marta suggestions as to how she might have handled the situation, Robert told her that she was not growing professionally and that he would have to let the principal know that her lack of control in the classroom was impeding the students' educational progress. In frustration, Marta accused Robert of using his role as mentor to get back at her for rebuffing him romantically.

Problems

Like the situation between Jordana and Harry, Marta and Robert's professional relationship was impaired when personal issues were raised. However, this case took an ugly turn when Robert and Marta were unable to resolve the situation and Robert, it seemed, was using his assigned role as mentor to make Marta's professional life difficult.

Marta honestly thought Robert was taking her rejection of his romantic overtures into the school building. Contrasting his behavior before and after the grant-writing day, Marta thought she could easily conclude that he was being arbitrarily difficult concerning her management questions, issues she had previously discussed with him with little concern about being "turned in" to the principal. After all, they had both reasoned that beginning teachers would inevitably have certain management issues as they became used to school policy, their own teaching style with individual students, and so on. However, that ease in discussion disappeared and Marta felt betrayed when Robert wanted to take his "concerns" about her classroom practices to the principal.

Robert, however, did not think he was acting in response to Marta's rejection of his advances. As a mentor, he knew he was responsible for helping Marta become a better teacher. When faced with what she admitted were continuing problems with classroom management, he thought he should make the principal aware in case parents complained that their students weren't learning in Marta's classroom.

Opportunities for Learning

Again, both cases outlined above would never have happened if the local administrators had followed the advice on same-gender pairing. Because they did not, we must consider the best reactions and solutions to the scenarios illustrated. First, the best advice to all educators is to remain professional. The second is to push all thoughts of workplace romance out of one's mind. That said, what advice can be given to both beginning and veteran teachers when the first two suggestions have been ignored?

Student teachers like Jordana may be more susceptible to workplace crushes simply because they're younger and have been living in an environment—college—that seems to encourage shifting from attraction to attraction. In addition, when student teachers spend a great deal of time with their mentors, they often develop a closeness as well as a reliance on them because the mentor has such an important role in the beginning teacher's life. If, in addition, they are placed with a mentor of the opposite gender—and one who may not be married—it may seem even less problematic to the student teacher to allow the attraction to become more serious.

Obviously, by the time Harry talked to the university supervisor, communication between the mentor and the student teacher had all but ended, leaving them both confused about their roles. The university supervisor who must deal with this kind of scenario has a number of options to consider. One is to move the student teacher out of the situation and place him or her with another teacher. This may be the only way to restore equanimity in the situation. Because the student teacher is a visitor in the classroom of the veteran teacher, the latter has a right to ask that the student teacher be moved, especially if there are concerns about the tension between the teachers affecting the students. If that option is chosen, the supervisor needs to move the student teacher to another school, make sure the new mentor is the same gender, and encourage the mentor to write a recommendation that focuses only on the student teacher's professional work in the classroom. The supervisor should also provide a recommendation that explains that the student teaching placement was split so that the student teacher could, for example, experience both middle and high school.

For those of you wondering if the supervisor or Harry should mention the attraction in a recommendation, we suggest that it not be done. In this case, there was no pattern of Jordana falling in love with a mentor figure and then making his life difficult because of it; consequently, bringing what may well be a one-time-only blunder could jeopardize Jordana's job chances in the future. The split assignment, however, will not.

A second option for Jordana and Harry would be to have Jordana stay with the placement but only after a conversation between the two teachers and the university supervisor to make clear that all involved know what they need to do to assure the necessary professional relationship. Included in this may need to be more visits from the university supervisor. Most important, though, the two teachers involved must create guidelines that each can live by for the rest of the student teaching experience. Planning issues—both individual and team—as well as other interactions between the two may need to be negotiated. In addition, the two teachers must talk about their concerns about working with each other honestly and openly, because this is their only recourse if they choose to continue the student teaching experience.

The situation between Marta and Robert may also benefit from the wisdom of other parties. It is clear that Marta does not trust Robert to continue in his capacity as mentor; indeed, Robert may find his life easier if he is not the person Marta must, in many ways, report to. Although it will take a great deal of courage on both teachers' part, they will need to go to the principal or whoever is in charge of the mentoring program at the school and ask for a change of mentor. How much detail they share with the principal or mentor supervisor is up to them. Furthermore, the administrator they talk to must respect how much the two teachers are willing to share, focusing on appreciating that they are mature people who know when a situation is not working to their mutual benefit. A new mentor assignment can be handled in this particular case by saying that Robert is simply too busy to continue successfully mentoring Marta and that a replacement should be considered. If it is close to the end of the school year, a new mentor might not even be needed. Or it may be more sensible to have the director of the mentor program take over the mentoring in the short term.

However, if Robert is, indeed, trying to sabotage Marta's career, or if others perceive that he is working against Marta, more specific steps must be taken. Again, Robert must be removed from the mentor relationship to protect both his and Marta's interests. The principal must be part of any discussion between the two and should be vigilant in trying to make sure that neither one is further damaged because of their new incompatibility in the workplace. If the school district is large enough, Marta or Robert might consider moving to a different educational site. If moving is not a possibility, the principal might suggest a change in rooms to create a greater physical distance between the two. He or she may also encourage the teachers to serve on different committees, make sure they do not have the same planning or lunch periods, and find another mentor to do formal or evaluative observations.

Affairs in the workplace can be disastrous for a number of reasons. For teachers these types of situations are especially hard on credibility. Because teachers are, for good or for bad, role models to their students, they should remain extra vigilant in keeping professional lives professional and personal lives outside the school building.

Matriarchal or Patriarchal Problems

When we combine issues of age and gender, we find a variety of opportunities for less than successful mentoring relationships. Matriarchal or patriarchal impositions on the mentoring relationship and gender misunderstandings where pedagogical differences are too different can create problems for even the most able teachers.

Clark had been teaching health and physical education for years at the elementary level; he was also a successful football coach at the local high school. When Mitch, a new teacher to the district, was assigned to him for mentoring, Clark took his role as seriously as he took the state football playoffs. He offered Mitch advice on how much time to spend planning for his classes, how many hours to give to his new assignment coaching junior varsity wrestling, how much energy to save for his off-hours. He asked Mitch to accompany him on scouting trips so that he could share his wisdom on "knowing the opponent" with his younger companion. He gave Mitch his full attention at lunch and commented to the younger man on how to best balance family obligations with coaching duties. However, when Clark came to the second wrestling match of the season, sat with Mitch on the bench, and offered him advice on promoting "that winning spirit" with the young wrestlers, Mitch knew he had had enough. But how could he get Clark to back off without hurting the older man's feelings?

Problem and Opportunity for Learning

This particular situation was solved primarily through honesty and resolve on Mitch's part. During his first weeks at his new job, Mitch was more than happy to have Clark to lean on. However, as he became more comfortable with his teaching and coaching assignments, Mitch realized that he needed to spend less time with Clark, mainly because the veteran teacher was taking up too much of the time Mitch needed for planning. Because he felt guilty doing that, though, Mitch ended up taking more work home with him than he should have, resulting in family problems. Specifically, Mitch needed to sit down with Clark, thank him for all he had done, and let him know he would continue to see Clark as someone to talk to as problems emerged. However, he also needed to be clear that he had things under control and needed to enjoy that success without trying to add more to his professional plate.

Issues may also arise when a younger but experienced teacher mentor is assigned to an older, nontraditional student teacher.

Grace, a forty-nine-year-old mother and wife, had returned to the college campus after a twenty-eight-year absence. Her classmates in the methods courses loved her because she brought cookies to class, sympathized with them like their mother would have if she'd been near, and was a role model of efficiency in all aspects of her work. Because she got along so well with her twentysomething classmates, there was little concern when the placement office put her with Max, a dynamic twenty-nine-year-old fifth-grade teacher. Although they got along wonderfully at the beginning of the semester and both found many positive aspects of the other's teaching style and abilities, tensions began to escalate when Grace began questioning Max about his out-of-school life. Max politely suggested to Grace that they should confine the subject of their conversations to the job, yet Grace persisted, telling Max she really wanted to know more about him. When Max finally gave in and shared some information about himself with her, Grace took it upon herself to give him advice about his girlfriend, his health, and anything else she deemed important. Eventually uncomfortable with the constant barrage of helpful advice, Max finally told Grace that they really would have to stick to discussing the classroom situation and nothing else. Grace backed off, but both felt that the professional relationship had been compromised by the tensions in the personal relationship. Their team planning time all but disappeared, and Grace felt a certain amount of animosity toward Max when he critiqued her planning choices and management skills.

Problems

Grace seemed to automatically default into an "I'm older and wiser" position within the relationship, focusing more on personal issues than professional ones. It is probably obvious that the "mother-to-son" role Grace adopted with Max was also connected to gender. Yet, clearly, Max was the teacher with the significant years of teaching experience, and he necessarily had to be the professional concerning classroom situations.

Opportunities for Learning

In both situations above, it is evident that when one of the members of the pairing attempts a patriarchal or matriarchal role, power becomes an issue. In our first scenario, Clark's power over Mitch forces the younger teacher to adapt his style in ways that align with Clark's way of defining teaching and coaching. If Mitch hadn't been able to assert himself, it might have taken a long time for him to find his own personality in the classroom and on the field. His frustration along the way might have caused him to rethink his choice of career.

In the situation with Max and Grace, Grace realizes that she cannot take on the "elder" professional role, so she takes on a mothering role, one with which she is familiar. Although she can offer various teaching ideas to Max, she is not in the power position she may be used to with her own family. Her need to define her place in the classroom and in her work with Max provides a quandary that she resolves by recreating the matriarchal situation she is used to at home.

Max may have even unwittingly supported this matriarchal approach through the simple respect he showed Grace in the beginning of their semester together. He may not have articulated certain expectations for Grace as a student teacher that he might have set with a younger beginning teacher.

Although the clash was inevitable in both situations, it doesn't necessarily mean that the relationships couldn't be repaired. In the case of Mitch and Clark, Clark took Mitch's telling him about needing his own professional time to heart, and both men continued to meet regularly at school. Their conversations became more balanced, and as the years passed, they truly became colleagues. This is a case of professionalism winning out, along with the good sense by both teachers to trust that mentoring and listening could occur as the beginning teacher asked for consultation or the mentor was reminded of an insight that would be helpful to the younger teacher.

Max and Grace also have the potential for reconciliation as Grace learns to respect the experience Max already has in the classroom. Max must also help Grace see that she has a great deal to offer to her colleagues. For example, veteran teachers can support less experienced colleagues by promoting them in as many professional capacities as feasible—conference attendance, membership on committees, involvement in extracurricular areas that highlight beginning teachers' abilities, and so on. They must also make sure they provide opportunities for both team and individual planning.

Another sensible reminder, and one we mentioned concerning attractions between teachers, is to keep the personal life personal. In our work with student teachers, we routinely encourage them not to share many aspects of their personal lives with their mentor teachers. Boyfriends, girlfriends, spouses, and problems with family members are all topics that do not need to enter the classroom. Although we understand that many beginning and veteran teachers become good friends, we encourage that to happen after the professional relationship has been established.

Summary

Every mentoring match-up has its unique characteristics. Issues of age and gender may affect the relationships teachers have with each other in both positive and negative ways. Our discussion of each of the following—colleagues too close in age or inexperience; colleagues too far apart in age; colleagues at different places in their careers; gender misunderstandings; having a gay or lesbian teacher in the equation; attraction between the beginning and mentor teacher; and matriarchal or patriarchal problems—allows us to consider how easily misunderstandings or misconceptions can negatively affect the mentoring relationship. Although personal misunderstandings may be the root of most problems, teachers must also be prepared to discuss differences in political stances or in communication styles. And although each member of the mentoring relationship must talk and collaborate with the other to heighten the understanding of what each person brings to the relationship and how that situation is enhanced by their different strengths, people outside the relationship, such as administrators or university supervisors, may also need to help alleviate challenges between the mentor and mentee. The key in all of these situations is for both members to remind themselves that they are in a professional relationship; as long as talk can center around classroom practice and professional insights, the relationship between educators should flourish.

Mentoring Across Culture

A n advanced ESL student tried to explain her conclusions about living in a culture that was different from her own to her teacher-mentor. "Laws are not that much different from one country to another, you know? You don't have that many problems understanding the laws when you move to a new place. You have trouble with all those rules that aren't written down." When we consider the issues that arise in mentoring partnerships involving teachers from different cultures working together, we have to agree with this ESL student: the problems tend to arise from misunderstanding the rules that aren't written down.

We are tempted to turn to a chapter such as this one in hopes of finding easily accessible formulas such as "Six Steps for Success in Cross-Cultural Partnerships," or charts contrasting the cultural characteristics of teachers from Hispanic, Caucasian, Asian American, African American, and Native American backgrounds. Unfortunately, such easy summaries are likely to oversimplify complex matters; the resulting pictures of the beliefs of the various cultures represented become caricatures rather than realistic portraits. This chapter looks at cross-cultural mentoring partnerships in more general terms, beginning with the account of the partnership between Sarah Charles and Erleen Begay. The names have been changed, but their story is a composite of the experiences of several mentors and the new professionals they have mentored. In it, we see many of the issues that can arise when teachers of differing cultural backgrounds work together.

Erleen Begay was pleased to be hired at Landmark Elementary School after her graduation from Southwestern State University. Ever since beginning her teacher-training program, she had hoped to work eventually at a school with a high percentage of Navajo students. As a Navajo professional herself, she wanted to inspire her sixth graders to a greater feeling of confidence and to assure them that they could tackle the educational system and emerge victorious.

That educational system had been a challenge for Erleen herself, despite her family's unwavering support and her own strong abilities. She'd been an excellent high school student at her small reservation school, in both athletics and academics, but the transition to college had been difficult for her. Although she earned respectable grades, the college culture, with its high percentage of Caucasian students, seemed difficult to penetrate. Erleen persevered, learned much, and eventually sailed through her student teaching under the supervision of an experienced Hispanic mentor teacher who had years of multicultural teaching experience. Because her student teaching experience had been so enriching, Erleen was delighted to learn that she would be assigned a professional teacher-mentor for her first year at Landmark. This colleague, she was told, would support and help her in her teaching and eventually assist her building principal in evaluating her performance.

Sarah Charles, a native of Georgia, felt equally delighted to be assigned the task of mentoring Erleen. She'd come to Landmark City after having taught for five years in a rural, primarily African American district in Georgia. Though Caucasian herself, she'd felt completely at home in the African American culture of her previous school and had few difficulties relating to her students there. Pleased by her record of success in working with an ethnic group different from her own, Landmark's administrators decided to hire her. Both Sarah and Erleen would have sixth-grade classes composed primarily of Navajo and Hispanic students.

Landmark's administrators thought that pairing these two teachers would benefit both of them. Erleen would be exposed to a multiculturally experienced teacher with strong skills, and Sarah would gain a wonderful resource for learning about her own Navajo students.

Three weeks after the start of the school year, Sarah arrived to observe Erleen for the first time. She had never seen a more relaxed classroom. When the bell rang, Erleen stood at the file cabinet, searching for a needed handout. Once she found it, she approached the front of the room, only to be stopped by a student who initiated a four-minute discussion of a missing assignment. When this conversation was finished, Erleen calmly focused the attention of the class and began to explain their next project for language arts. Students questioned one another and Erleen to clarify their understanding. They were obviously as calm and at ease as Erleen herself. Yet, watching from her seat in the back of the room, Sarah felt restless. Where was the forward movement, the urgency, that characterizes a good class? It's true that everything seemed to get done eventually, but the clock was running, and Sarah thought progress was far too slow for the optimal classroom pace.

At recess time, Sarah and Erleen met to discuss the observation. "You need to grab their attention right away," Sarah suggested. "Make sure you're ready the moment the bell rings—get started right away. Pick up the pace of the lesson." Erleen listened with apparent interest, took extensive notes, and thanked Sarah for her time and her input. Sarah felt affirmed. She decided that she loved working with a new teacher and making a difference in her professional life.

Two weeks later, Sarah came in to observe Erleen again. She was first surprised, then angry, and finally exasperated to realize that everything in Erleen's class proceeded exactly as it had in the first observation. The pace was still slow, and students were still calm and pleasantly, but not urgently, engaged in the business of the class. Erleen still allowed herself to be interrupted by students with questions, no matter when they were asked. Assuming that Erleen had somehow misunderstood her suggestions, Sarah suggested an alternative strategy: that Erleen come and observe her class. Erleen agreed to do so.

Later in the week, Erleen slipped into the teacher's chair at the side of the room while Sarah called her own class to order. About five minutes into the class, a student warily entered the room. "Take your seat and get out your language arts book," Sarah told him bluntly. "Don't let this happen again. You've been late twice before, and we don't put up with that kind of behavior in this classroom." Erleen was amazed at the rapid-fire pace of Sarah's lesson, and wondered whether some of the students were being left behind. Most students, however, seemed to be following with interest. Sarah ran a teacher-centered morning session—there was little discussion, questioning, or collaboration as she outlined the work for the day. Students who seemed distracted were quickly called back to task. Sarah spoke and acted quickly, moving from one topic to the next with little pause. Within a few minutes, the students had books and papers out and the first assignment started. Sarah approached Erleen. "See what I mean about pace?" she asked. "There's no time wasted in here."

"Thanks for letting me observe," Erleen replied with a smile. "I think I'll be getting back to my room now. I don't want to impose on Mrs. Jimenez to watch my students any longer. Talk to you later."

Sarah sensed that behind Erleen's smile and her thanks, something was not quite right. She had hoped Erleen would stay longer and observe more extensively. However, Sarah thought, at least she saw the way I start the day. That should help her get things moving faster in her room.

That afternoon, across town at Southwestern State, university supervisor Kent Relton, who had supervised Erleen's student teaching, received a phone call. "May I talk to you after school today?" Erleen asked. "I think I have a little problem here."

By four o'clock, Erleen was in Kent's office. "I don't know what to do about my mentor teacher," she explained. "She's nice in lots of ways, but she doesn't understand our Navajo students at all. She wants me to teach like she teaches, and I just can't. All that rushing and hustling and hurrying—that isn't me, and it isn't the way to reach our students. She seems so rude in the classroom, singling out people if they do something wrong and scolding them in front of others. She talks so fast; I don't think the students are taking in half of what she says. I couldn't do that—it isn't right. Why would I even want to teach like that? I try to be polite and listen to her, but I can't do what she says if I think it is wrong." Erleen paused. "Here's the biggest problem, though. She is going to help write my evaluation. I need this job. I can't afford to lose it over something like this. What should I do?"

Kent secured Erleen's permission to visit Landmark and confer with Sarah. Sarah was pleased to have the opportunity to report the problems she saw with Erleen's instruction. "It takes her forever to get anything done in the classroom, Dr. Relton. She's nice, and she's smart, and you can see that the students love her—but she is wasting so much time. She needs to be a stronger leader, that's for sure."

Kent listened attentively to Sarah's comments. "You have a lot of responsibility this year, Sarah. How are things going for you at Landmark? Are you enjoying your teaching this year?"

Sarah paused before answering. "Well, yes—and no. I'm really frustrated by attendance issues. So many of my students miss school too much, especially the Navajo children. How can they learn if they aren't here consistently? Then, in class, I'm often hearing students give the excuse that they didn't understand what they were supposed to do, even when I've explained the assignment thoroughly. I don't know how to be any clearer."

"Have you asked Erleen about the attendance issue? I know that sometimes Navajo families have ceremonial responsibilities that cause the children to be absent on occasion. Perhaps she could clarify the issue for you."

"Ceremonial responsibilities? But school is in session. It's one thing to keep children at home if they are sick, but to go to a ceremony? Children do not succeed in this world because they've been to every ceremony—only if they've done well in school," Sarah replied heatedly.

"Well, yes, I understand what you mean, Sarah. That certainly is the prevailing wisdom. You may find that some of your students and their families feel differently about that, however. Erleen might be able to help you understand their viewpoint."

"Their viewpoint simply needs to change, as I see it," Sarah asserted. "There's no point in understanding it—it needs to be changed."

Two months later, at a district meeting, Kent met Ana Ricardo, the principal of Landmark Elementary School. She told him she was concerned about his former student, Erleen. Erleen's mentor, Sarah, thought she was not strong enough in the classroom. "How does Sarah herself seem to be doing?" Kent asked.

"She's very competent, though several parents have called to say that their children have trouble understanding their assignments. They say she moves too fast for the students."

Kent was concerned. He had seen a few cross-cultural mentoring partnerships end poorly in the past and he was afraid that this partnership also had the potential to conclude badly despite the best intentions of both teachers. "It would be very helpful if the two of them could talk more freely," he suggested. Ana agreed. "I'll keep working with them."

Despite the principal's best efforts, however, the misunderstandings between Sarah and Erleen continued through the school year, never breaking out into outright hostility, but never resolving into genuine understanding or true collegiality. Erleen continued to think Sarah was closed to the needs and preferred learning styles of the school's ethnic minorities, and Sarah continued to think Erleen's less urgent style in the classroom demonstrated a lack of leadership and strength. By the end of the school year, they avoided each other actively, and mutual observation and assistance had stopped. When new teachers were evaluated for retention at year's end, Sarah's assessment of Erleen was extremely low, partly because of the issue of leadership and partly because Erleen had not changed her performance in response to Sarah's comments. Ana suspected that this was not quite fair to Erleen, but she knew that Sarah had observed Erleen much more often than she had. Erleen was offered a contract for the following year, but placed on professional probation at Landmark. Erleen decided to accept a teaching offer from another school instead. During the summer, the results of the sixth-grade standardized tests arrived in the principal's office. Ana was both surprised by and rueful at the resulting scores. Both Erleen's class and Sarah's showed excellent—and very similar—rates of improvement.

Erleen and Sarah's story reflects many of the problems that can arise during cross-cultural partnerships. Understanding these problems is not just a theoretical concern. The United States census prediction says that ethnic minority groups will make up 47 percent of the population by 2050 (Aragon 2000, p. 2). Teachers in some districts face astonishing cultural and linguistic diversity in their classrooms already. College enrollments across all majors, including education, reflect the trend toward increasingly multicultural student bodies. Educational surveys, however, show that change is slower to affect actual teacher populations. Although both mentors and new professionals may come from previously subordinated groups in some urban schools, the majority—approximately 75 percent—of experienced U.S. teachers are Caucasian, generally female, and usually middle class (Hoffman 2003, p. 27). However, the beginning teachers in need of mentoring show far more diversity as a group. As a consequence, cross-cultural mentoring partnerships nationally tend to be like Sarah and Erleen's pairing: combining an experienced Caucasian teacher and a beginning teacher from a differing ethnic and cultural background.

When operating at their best, such partnerships can open the richest vistas for each participant. Each may benefit through exposure to another teaching style and another worldview. Unfortunately, such partnerships also offer fertile ground for misunderstanding between participants, and can be difficult for both parties, as we saw in Sarah and Erleen's case.

Developing a Successful Cross-Cultural Mentoring Relationship

One Hispanic teacher reflected on her search for helpful mentoring in a largely Caucasian setting in this vivid way:

> *If one is a minority in the education field, and if one wants to be mentored, one has to accept what guidance one can from Anglos, and swallow a lot of pride and gloss over a lot of thoughtless mistakes, or at least not allow one's anger to rule one's work performance or the relationship with the mentor. It can be done, but I find I must be constantly on guard lest I say something to dismay the gringos. When someone does make a stupid comment, I have to chew my tongue off before responding. Someone . . . once asked me, with great sincerity, "Why do Hispanic women have so many babies out of wedlock?" I had to take a couple of deep breaths before pointing out that my mother gave birth to three daughters in wedlock and none without, that my little sister had given birth to her first son after eight years of marriage and the second after ten years, and that I had no babies at*

all, in or out of wedlock. Remind me to show you the chew marks on the insides of my cheeks sometime.

Though it is important to keep in mind that most cross-cultural partnerships are successful, a consideration of some of the issues that can affect these types of relationships are important for both administrators and potential mentors to acknowledge before placements are made. In essence, we consider the following to be necessary attributes in creating and sustaining cross-cultural mentoring relationships:

- a willingness to work with members of other cultures and ethnicities;
- an eagerness to acquire knowledge about others' cultural backgrounds;
- an ability to understand that knowledge and pedagogy may be culturally conditioned; and
- an open attitude toward talking to one's mentoring partner honestly about cultural issues.

A Willingness to Work with Members of Other Cultures and Ethnicities

An open and willing attitude is, of course, the first requirement toward mentoring successfully in a cross-cultural situation. Fortunately, because of their characteristic concern for others, many teachers tend to be liberal in this way. However, it is commonly assumed that where this openness is present, no problems will arise. This belief is likely to be naïve, as we see in Sarah and Erleen's case. Each of them positively relished the opportunity to work with the other, yet misunderstandings occurred that ultimately damaged the mentoring relationship.

Although it is true that teachers from divergent cultural backgrounds share important common values, such as a concern for the welfare and education of their students, how they realize these beliefs in the classroom may be quite different. One teacher may feel strongly, as Erleen did, that scolding individual students in front of classmates is entirely unacceptable, whereas another, like Sarah, thinks it is vital to do so in order to make clear to all students that misbehavior has unpleasant consequences. Cultural differences have thus entered the classroom in a way that threatens the basic pedagogical stance of both teachers. How will they resolve these differences? If one

teacher is a mentor and one a student teacher, the mentor can usually maintain her stance because of the difference in authority. This may make the student teacher unhappy, but the situation may at least be contained for the
duration of the student teaching. However, when one teacher is a professional mentor to a colleague, especially if the mentor has evaluative responsibilities as in Sarah and Erleen's case, the situation can present significant
difficulties.

Most authorities in educational mentoring stress the importance of sepa-
rating the tasks of mentoring and evaluation. This is particularly vital in
cross-cultural partnerships. Beginning teachers who know their mentors will
also be evaluating performance may not feel free to share concerns with
them. Similarly, mentors may feel the need to act as if no problems ever enter
their classroom doors—that they must project an image of unfailing competence if they are the evaluating authorities. Obviously, this is destructive of
the mentor/mentee relationship.

An Eagerness to Acquire Knowledge About Others' Cultural Backgrounds

Marguerite had served as a mentor to a number of beginning teachers, but when her
principal asked her to take on the newest addition to the school, Marguerite had to
stop and think a moment before saying yes. Saburo was originally from Japan and
had taught for a number of years in a Japanese boys' preparatory school in Tokyo.
Although Marguerite knew about Japan and had a general sense of its educational
approaches, she suspected that Saburo would find a move to the southern United
States a very different experience and that this, in turn, would create a real challenge for whoever accepted the offer to mentor him.

After her initial hesitation faded, though, Marguerite found herself on a new mission: to find out as much about Japanese teacher training, schools, and cultural attitudes about education as she could. Thankful for the search engine on her
computer, she began looking for information that would help ground her mentoring
as she began working with Saburo.

Beyond a willingness to work with a member of another ethnic group,
mentors must be eager to acquire knowledge about the cultural background
of the mentored teacher. If your new student teacher comes from Syria, for

example, what do you know about that culture? How can you find out? Are you willing to make the effort? One implied attitude of many prospective cross-cultural mentors is "we're all the same under the skin and if we just keep this in mind, there will be no problems." There is a kernel of truth here—people from every culture are similar in that they love their families, desire a safe life with opportunities for their children to progress, and admire beauty, truth, and high ideals. Beyond these overarching similarities, though, we are not all the same. For example, the ways in which we express love for our families vary enormously, with some cultures expressing their feelings openly and others with great reserve. Likewise, although the admiration of beauty may be universal, the definition of beauty changes remarkably from one cultural group to the next.

Then, there is the place of the individual within the culture. If every member of each ethnic group displayed uniform and predictable behaviors, cross-cultural partnerships would be easy to establish and sustain. However, each member of society inhabits two overlapping spheres of influence. Cultural and ethnic background is one such sphere. Diverse cultural groups do display certain general traits that distinguish them from others. However, innate individual personality traits, upbringing, education, and experiences form a second sphere of influence. It is extremely difficult to accurately assess the reasons for the behaviors of our mentors or mentees. Does Erleen's calm, unhurried, soft-spoken conduct relate to her Navajo heritage and nurture? Or is it simply a hallmark of Erleen's own personality, as biologically innate as her brown eyes? Sarah doesn't know, so she is uncertain how to address the effect it has on Erleen's teaching.

The teacher you mentor may or may not match your stereotyped norm for her cultural or ethnic group—any more than you match yours. Knowledge means not only learning about the cultural background of the teacher you mentor, but also understanding that teacher as an individual within a larger cultural group.

An Ability to Understand That Knowledge and Pedagogy May Be Culturally Conditioned

Another important attribute of successful mentors is recognizing that there are differences in our underlying assumptions about how the world works and the manner in which each of us functions within it. We tend to assume that on some level, everyone shares the same basic ideas about how the world operates, whether inside or outside the classroom. But completely rational, well-meaning individuals may not share these beliefs at all. Let's look at a lighthearted example from a high school class that illustrates a major difference in assumptions, this time between teacher and student.

A discussion arose in Joan Phillips's ESL classroom about what the various cultural groups represented in the class did with young children's lost teeth. Joan, a Caucasian teacher, talked about the prevalence in the United States of the tooth-fairy tale and its accompanying exchange of money for the lost tooth. A Laotian student described the custom in his village of standing in the doorway of the house with feet exactly even, and throwing the tooth into the yard.

"Why do you have to have your feet exactly even?" Joan asked casually.

"Because if your feet are just right, then the new tooth comes in perfectly straight, but if your feet are crooked when you throw the old tooth, the new one will be crooked, too."

"But this is like the tooth-fairy story, right?" Joan asked. "People do it, but they don't believe it really, do they?"

The student looked at her in surprise. "I believe this."

The teacher persisted. "Scientifically, though, there wouldn't be any reason why the position of your feet would have anything to do with your teeth."

"Well, who has straighter teeth, you or me?" asked the student, smiling broadly to show his beautifully aligned teeth.

"But what you did couldn't have caused your teeth to be straight," Joan replied.

"Why not?" asked the student.

"Because it isn't scientific," Joan began again. Abruptly she laughed. "We aren't going to agree in this case, are we?"

In this discussion, the teacher persists in her assumptions (not unreasonably, given her scientific knowledge) and the student persists in his (not unreasonably, given his evidence and experience). In this case, because their relationship was strong, friendly, and open, some education took place on both sides and no harm was done. But the participants in the discussion were each certain that they were right, both during the discussion and afterward. They assumed that there could be no rational opposition to their viewpoint and that anyone who differed from them was simply wrong. This type of difference in assumptions is often the heart of cross-cultural mentoring difficulties as well.

In Sarah and Erleen's story, Sarah assumes that any good class gets off to a strong start as soon as the bell rings. In this, she is supported by much of the pedagogical literature. But there is a profoundly significant reason why the literature backs Sarah's position: most of today's pedagogical literature was written by Caucasian teachers. Erleen is appalled and embarrassed by what she sees as Sarah's rudeness in the classroom. In fact, she is so turned off by Sarah's technique that she is disinclined to hear any more of what Sarah has to say as a mentor. In this, Erleen is supported by her own cultural assumption that singling out individual students for either reprimands or praise is unwise and inappropriate. In the end, standardized testing reveals that the two classes made similar—and impressive—gains during the school year. Obviously, each technique worked for the teacher who was employing it. Neither approach was universally right or wrong. Yet the results of the mentoring pairing became negative because each teacher stood by her assumption of right and wrong and refused to acknowledge that the other teacher might also be teaching effectively, though differently.

To mentor effectively in a cross-cultural situation, we must be willing to admit that there is more than one way to teach well. We must be willing to see that our standards of good pedagogy are culturally conditioned, also—and not necessarily the only effective way to teach. We must be willing to put our educational cards on the table and discuss our differences, tactfully but honestly.

An Open Attitude Toward Talking to One's Mentoring Partner Honestly About Cultural Issues

Ask a group of people in the United States about "political correctness" and you'll probably get a variety of reactions as to why it's necessary and why it's detrimental. Discussing issues that might be considered politically (in)correct can create its own tensions in the mentoring relationship. Unfortunately, there is no easy formula for this type of discussion. It is possible that your introduction of cultural differences may be initially misunderstood by your mentoring partner, especially if that partner comes from a minority group that has traditionally been oppressed by Caucasian culture. Yet, if we are to avoid the type of situation in which Sarah and Erleen found themselves, the discussions must be initiated if possible. Even here, it is important to keep in mind that the positive value of frank and honest discussion is, to a great

extent, a Caucasian notion. Some cultures value subtlety rather than open, blunt communication. These cultures adopt the position that forcing someone to bare his or her innermost feelings is a socially inappropriate demand.

The best time to deal with cross-cultural issues is before they arise so that they are not linked to performance. For instance, when meeting Erleen, Sarah might have said, "I'm new in the Southwest and don't have any experience with Navajo or Hispanic cultures, but I really want to learn. Would you please give me any suggestions that you think might help me? And please mention it if you see me inadvertently do or say anything that is culturally inappropriate." This would at least have opened the door for Erleen to be able to raise cultural issues and would have signaled to her that such interventions would be welcome, not offensive.

Hinting at issues is rarely a successful technique where cross-cultural partnerships are concerned, as Sarah discovered. Despite the value placed upon subtle interactions by some cultures, the slow process of allowing a point to be made by repeated hints is a luxury most classroom work does not allow. It is probably better to be straightforward, though polite. A statement such as, "Each time I've observed your class, I've noticed that you begin the day slowly and casually instead of jumping right in with plans and activities. Help me understand your reasons for starting the day in this way" might have opened the discussion effectively while remaining respectful of Erleen's methods and choices.

Remaining humble and teachable is difficult when our basic assumptions about good teaching are being questioned or threatened. It is often easier to accuse a mentoring partner of incompetence or prejudice than to relax our assumptions and consider another viewpoint. Yet all of us need to see a cross-cultural mentoring partnership not as a problem but as an opportunity to learn from someone who may approach things differently than we do and has much to teach us.

Summary

Developing cross-cultural mentoring relationships may be one of the trickiest tasks two teachers ever have to navigate. Even with the best of intentions, mentors and mentees may inadvertently miscommunicate their needs or intentions, often resulting in misunderstandings and hard feelings. Considering some of the issues that can affect these types of mentoring relationships is

important for both administrators and potential mentors to acknowledge before placements are made. In this chapter, then, we consider the following attributes and how they promote the creation of and support for cross-cultural mentoring relationships.

The first attribute, a willingness to work with members of other cultures and ethnicities, is primary in gauging whether certain individuals can even be assigned to a mentoring situation. It is usually easy to spot someone who will not work well with a person of another cultural background because of their language choices or interactions with certain students or colleagues. A spoken willingness is an important first step, but that must be coupled with the potential mentor's eagerness to acquire knowledge about others' cultural backgrounds; this interest can manifest itself in a variety of ways. The mentor may do his or her own research or seek out experts who know the particular traditions or expectations of a specific culture.

Once those first attributes have been established, it is important that the mentor have the ability to understand that knowledge and pedagogy may be culturally conditioned. This means that the mentor understands the need for flexibility in observing and discussing the various pedagogical choices a beginning teacher may make, especially a novice from a cultural background different from the mentor's. Ideally, this flexibility will be additionally manifested through open and honest dialogues with one's mentoring partner about cultural issues so that both teachers can better understand their pedagogical choices as well as how culture and prior experience affect our choices as professionals.

Mentoring in Rural or Urban Schools

with Robert Petrone and Sandra Raymond

The United States is facing a significant teacher shortage, especially in rural and urban schools. Urban areas with a demographic of largely minority students often have limited funds for teacher salaries, classroom resources and teaching materials, and maintenance of school grounds. Rural sites face similar economic problems and may be less attractive to teachers interested in a social life at the end of the professional day.

This chapter deals specifically with (1) the problems and issues that can create an enormous amount of stress for new teachers in urban or rural school settings and (2) how important mentoring is in supporting beginning teachers who find themselves in schools culturally, economically, and socially different from those in which they were brought up or they experienced in their student teaching.

A Rural Experience

Julie locked her car, got out, and stood in the parking lot of P-V-C Consolidated High School. The school was a large, seventy-year-old brick structure with a run-down combination football field/track on its grounds. At twenty-two, Julie had just finished a successful student teaching experience in newly remodeled Meadow Middle School, a suburban school close to the university she had attended. Born and raised in suburbia, Julie considered her new job a necessary challenge in her development as a professional. She knew that rural schools had a difficult time finding teachers, especially math teachers, and she had been impressed with the way the principal and his staff had talked about the school and the neighboring communities that made up the school district. In the glow of the successful feeling of the interview, Julie hadn't looked too carefully at the building, her classroom, or the computer labs she considered necessary to provide her students the technology background she considered important in math education "for the future."

Meeting her mentor, Jefferson, on the first day of the teacher inservice provided some insights into her new teaching environment. As Jefferson talked, Julie began to better understand the positives as well as the challenges of the rural site. "Well, we probably don't have as current a computer lab as you're used to, but there are enough computers for a class of twenty, and since most of yours have twelve to sixteen students, you won't have access problems. And there is Internet service on the computer in your classroom. I'm sure you'll be able to make do. Now, what else do you have questions or concerns about?"

Beginning teachers often have questions about their new school and the facilities available. In some cases, beginning teachers in rural facilities find that the technology and/or equipment they took for granted in the schools they attended or in which they student taught is simply not available. Indeed, some school districts in Arizona, for example, still don't have Internet access because there is only one phone line into the school site. In situations like these, it is imperative that the mentor help the novice teacher think creatively, considering ways to make education work within the constraints of available technology.

Jefferson's approach was helpful to Julie in the sense that she could quickly understand the current limitations on the technology while appreciating the fact that with some forethought on her part, she would have no problems having students work independently or in pairs on available computers.

Introducing New Teachers to Community/School Sites in the District

Over lunch on the second day of the inservice, Jefferson asked if Julie had had a chance to check out the various towns that made up P-V-C. "Actually, I hadn't even thought about it. I know that Preston is the largest of the three towns. . . ." Julie stopped in embarrassment; it had never occurred to her that she might want to know the communities in which her students lived. After all, they were all lower- and middle-class white students, weren't they?

"Well, actually, there are four towns now; when they added Filmont, they didn't add the F because the cheerleaders already have a good rhythm with chants for the P-V-C." Jefferson chuckled. "If you've got time today after school, I'd be happy to drive you around; we could also stop and take a look at the middle school over in Vale and the elementary schools in Chernowith and Filmont. That way, when you start meeting people tomorrow in the full staff meeting, you'll be able to start making connections between names and schools, faces and teachers."

As they drove the fifty-mile radius of the school district later that day, Julie marveled at the differences in the four towns. Preston, at a population of 1,500, had a lively main street with a number of attractive storefronts and a definite feeling of bustle, thanks to the locally owned furniture factory that employed almost 400 people from the surrounding areas. Vale and Chernowith could have been mirrors of each other: both were extremely small farming communities with large grain cooperatives run by Farm Service. Neither had a grocery store, and the main streets in both towns were generally run-down, typically featuring a bar, a post office, two or three small churches, and a convenience store. Filmont, the latest add-on to P-V-C, had a population of 800, many of whom were minorities, and a turkey-processing plant on the edge of town.

Jefferson's running dialogue about the problems as well as the compromises made by the various schools to make P-V-C "work" was very informative for Julie. His assessment of how the curriculum of the school was undergoing another change to better accommodate the students from Filmont was extremely useful for the beginning teacher. In addition, the time outside school helped Julie feel like she was getting to know her colleague both personally and professionally, and she appreciated that, she decided later, more than anything.

Providing beginning teachers with a sense of their surroundings is extremely important when they are working in rural schools, especially in consolidated districts where students come from a number of communities and the farms or ranches in between. Jefferson was able to facilitate his drive around the district fairly easily; other mentors in larger-area districts, like those in the American West where one-way bus trips from the edge of the district boundary may be 100 miles, may need to use maps and visuals to help novice teachers understand the variety of environments from which students come. Regardless of how the "trip" is made, though, it is important to talk with beginning teachers about the interconnectedness of schools and communities in the school district.

Lack of Mentoring in the Content Area

As a mentor, Jefferson was almost all that Julie could have asked for: he knew the school district and the communities from which their students came, he made time to talk with her about successes and challenges, and he helped her negotiate the various political situations in their small district. However, Jefferson was a history teacher—he often joked that his mother had set him on that path when she named him—and knew little about a math curriculum. Although he could always provide supporting comments about management issues or collegial approaches, he couldn't provide much assistance when it came to math content. And because Julie was the only math teacher at the three-year high school, she had no one to turn to in the building when she had questions about her effectiveness.

Julie tried to secure content-area mentoring by contacting her counterpart at the middle school. Although Ramon tried to be helpful and he and Julie met a few times, scheduling difficulties made it virtually impossible for him to come over and watch Julie teach, especially because the middle school was in Vale, a twenty-minute drive from Preston. The principals of each school, sympathetic to Julie's situation, arranged for Ramon to come to the high school for a half-day observation in late October, but also let the teachers know that this was probably a onetime occurrence.

As we've noted in this book as well as *Mentoring Beginning Teachers,* most beginning teachers deem content-area or grade-level mentoring extremely important. In many rural situations, however, there may be one content-area teacher per school, making this type of mentoring virtually impossible. Julie and Ramon's attempts at some mentoring are commendable, but when this proves untenable, as was the situation at P-V-C because of travel and time constraints, beginning teachers may need to look into alternative ways of receiving mentoring in their subject areas, such as the following:

- on-line mentoring (Chapter 11) with former professors, teachers, or classmates,

- summer workshops that may provide additional support for content-area teachers, and

- additional coursework—possibly taken on-line, depending on college offerings.

Overabundance of Preparations and Extracurricular Activities

"OK, girls, pick up the tempo here; the routine is dragging!" yelled Julie to the varsity cheerleading squad. The girls moved in response to her words, but Julie wasn't sure she had given them much help. She had been thrown into the cheerleading sponsorship during her third week at P-V-C when the original coach, a local woman who also ran a dance academy, decided to move 300 miles away to the state capital, where she thought she would have more opportunities to dance as well as run a school. No one else had volunteered by the following Friday, and the cheerleading squad came to Julie in desperation. Even after she told them she had no experience, they continued to wheedle, promising that she wouldn't have to do much since they were already trained. It turned out that what they really needed was an adviser on the bus with them when they traveled to away games. So Julie agreed.

Now, with football season behind her and basketball and wrestling seasons looming, Julie realized what a huge mistake she had made. Along with her five academic preps, she would be spending every Tuesday, Wednesday, Friday, and Saturday with the cheering squad. Although she could bring work with her on the bus, it was hard to do much grading while sitting on the bleachers.

When she complained to Jefferson about all the time she was spending with the cheerleaders, he readily commiserated. During his first year, he, too, had had five preps and had been expected to be an assistant coach on both the football and baseball teams. He had also been assigned to be the junior class sponsor, which meant he was responsible for fund-raising.

"How did you survive?" asked Julie.

"I barely did!" said Jefferson. "I was able to step out of the baseball commitment when I found an area dad who was interested in working with the team. But as you know, I still haven't shed the other two. It's one of the biggest problems at small schools—finding enough people to cover all of the extracurriculars. Of course, we're so well compensated for all of our time." He smiled.

"So what can I do? I'm really feeling stressed about everything I've got to do. The cheerleading wouldn't be so bad if it wasn't practically every night."

"You might see if any of the mothers are willing to go. Seriously, Mrs. Davies works for the school, so I would think she'd qualify as a school chaperone."

"Anything is worth a try at this point. Thanks, Jefferson."

Combine extracurricular activities with the typical three to five preparations many rural teachers face and we can easily see how a situation like
Julie's escalates. Most of us have had similar situations, regardless of school
size, but it is not uncommon for teachers at rural sites to be responsible for
three or more sponsorships.

Little can be done about the number of preparations; however, principals,
mentors, and beginning teachers can employ certain strategies concerning
beginning teachers' extracurricular assignments:

- Principals must do a better job of not recruiting beginning teachers to take
  on extracurricular activities. Beginning teachers have so much to deal
  with in planning for their courses and assessing assignments that asking
  them to take on additional time commitments can only be detrimental to
  their success in the classroom. When the novice has agreed to take on an
  extra activity as part of his or her original contract, the administrator
  should consider, for example, giving the teacher an extra preparation
  period instead of assigning a study hall.

- Beginning teachers must also be stronger in saying no to these requests.
  Ten years ago, beginning teachers thought they had to agree to large
  numbers of preparations or two or three extracurricular activities to get a
  job. That reality does not exist in the current state of education. Although
  we are not advocating that beginning teachers negotiate their job description to nothing, we do encourage beginning teachers to be responsible
  about what they can accomplish successfully.

- Mentors can be especially effective in bolstering the courage of novice
  teachers as they refuse such assignments during their first year. As we
  have noted in other chapters in this book, mentors may create opportunities to talk with colleagues or administrators about the possible abuse of a
  beginning teacher's time and effort. When novices fail to stand up for
  themselves and their students begin to suffer, the mentor teacher has a
  responsibility to offer suggestions that will better support the beginning
  teacher during those first years.

Little or No Social Life

As she neared the end of her first year of teaching, Julie reflected on the positives—
Jefferson, her students, the staff at the school—as well as the challenges—little con-

tent-area mentoring, often inadequate resources, especially when it came to technology, the amount of time spent on extracurriculars—that the year had brought. Then there was the issue of her personal life, or rather, lack thereof.

Right before she took the job at P-V-C, Julie had broken up with her boyfriend, Tim. During the first months in Preston, Julie hadn't thought too much about missing a social life. After all, she had dated Tim two of the four years she had been at the university and had never been a big partyer. And Jefferson and other colleagues at the high school had been exceptional about including her in group activities connected to the school or local institutions.

But after going home for Christmas and seeing a number of her friends, Julie began to think about what she was missing by being so far from her "previous" life. She really hadn't made any friends outside the school, and because P-V-C was almost three hours away from a city where she might attend a Broadway road show or go to the symphony, Julie's whole life had been bound up in the school.

"There's actually nothing wrong with that, you know," said Jefferson when she told him about it. "Most beginning teachers really do need to focus on their teaching the first year. I was engaged myself, and my fiancée was a huge distraction." Jefferson laughed. "Seriously, she would get so mad at me because I wasn't paying enough attention to the wedding plans—to her. We actually broke up for about three weeks when I told her we wouldn't be able to get married if I lost my job. It was tough for a while. She was still in college and wasn't facing the time commitments that I was. It was much easier the next year after she had graduated and she had a job, too. Then she was the first-year teacher, and she understood more clearly why I hadn't been able to focus my attention on our life together very effectively."

"But at least you had the fiancée," Julie said. "Where am I going to find one out here?"

"We can work on that. If you'd told me that you were looking for a boyfriend. . . ."

"Actually, Jefferson, it's more than that. I miss going out with friends, shopping in a mall. I know it all sounds kind of silly, but I actually find shopping relaxing. And I'm finding that it's so . . . quiet out here. I'm not sure I'm cut out for rural life."

There are many reasons people choose to live in rural settings. The peace and quiet, possible outdoor activities, or returning to the small-town life one remembers from childhood are just a few. Teachers may look to rural communities for smaller class sizes and less bureaucracy. However, for teachers who have grown up in more suburban or urban settings, the shift from an urban to a rural lifestyle may include a great deal of culture shock.

- Some teachers with whom we talked said they "needed" the consistent exposure to museums and theater to be happy. With a somewhat embarrassed smile, Pam noted that the local theater, twenty miles from her school site, rarely offered movies during their first run and never offered independent films. In addition, as an art teacher, she would have loved to take her students to an art museum. "During my student teaching," she said, "we hopped in a bus and took a fifteen-minute drive to the city's museum of modern art. If I wanted to do that with my high school students, I'd have to plan an overnight trip with chaperones, hotels. It's just too much for me to consider at this point in my career."

- Many teachers noted the lack of intellectual support they had counted on at the university. Many rural sites are two to four hours away from university settings, so taking classes during the school year—once the beginning teacher is not so beginning anymore—is not an option. Although some universities have begun to invest in "distance education," either through Internet or television courses, many teachers find these types of classes less pedagogically sound than face-to-face offerings or simply do not have the technology necessary to make them work.

- Another bemoaned how long it took to drive places where there would be some social life. Vic said, "I don't want my students or their parents to see me out in the bars. I teach third grade and am very well aware that even though I'm old enough to drink in public, many of my parents wouldn't appreciate seeing me do that. Plus, I coach, and I'm afraid that I would run into my student athletes, requiring me to report them to the principal. It's not even like I'm a big drinker, but it would be nice to have the option of going out if I felt like it." This is a common problem for many younger beginning teachers, as they try to balance personal choices against townspeople's expectations of teachers.

- Some also feel that they cannot do without the variety of ethnic or regional foods—found either in restaurants or grocery stores—that have become very commonplace in more-populated areas. "It didn't even occur to me that I would miss Thai and Indian food so much," said Lon. "And it's not just the lack of restaurants; I can't even make it myself because there's no grocery that stocks most of what I need for 270 miles. I realize this seems pretty insignificant, but on days that I'm feeling sorry for myself, this just adds to my general feelings of gloom."

Jefferson and his colleagues did all the right things for Julie. They welcomed her into the communities themselves as well as the school community. They invited her to social events and made sure she had something to do on many weekends. (Of course, whether a mentor wants to find his mentee a boyfriend is purely a personal matter between the two of them.) After more discussion with Julie, Jefferson recommended that she return to the university for the summer and take courses toward a master's degree. This could accomplish two goals: becoming more confident of the content she was teaching and accessing a potential social life.

However, mentors cannot be expected to work miracles. Julie decided to return to P-V-C for a second year, but some beginning teachers may simply find that rural life is not for them.

An Urban High School

With visions of sharing with high school students the experiences of the characters of Thornton Wilder's *Our Town* or Holden Caulfield's desperate meanderings through the streets of Manhattan racing through his mind, Travis accepted his first teaching position at Franklin High School, an inner-city school. The area around Franklin, notorious for its gang activity, was plagued by violence, low socioeconomic status, and overall impoverished living conditions. Just a year before Travis arrived at the school, a student had been gunned down at the 7-11 store adjacent to the school, and the school maintained a steady 34 percent graduation rate.

Greeted by a façade of graffiti in a language Travis learned during his own high school days back in a fairly homogeneous, middle-class suburb of Long Island, New York, he maintained his smile and enthusiasm even after anxiously finding his way to the main office through the swarm of students—the vast majority of whom were Hispanic and speaking Spanish. Most paid him no attention, but some stared at him, smiled wryly, and spoke to their companions in Spanish, which usually elicited a laugh from the other onlookers. Finally finding the office, he soon discovered that there were no class sets of books or other materials for him, no syllabus or district curriculum guide to follow, and, despite the fact that he had been offered the job the day before and the school year was already eight weeks under way, he would have to start teaching tomorrow. "OK," he thought optimistically, "I guess I get to pick the books I want the students to read—*Our Town, Catcher in the Rye, The Color Purple.* . . ." Even the fact that he had to teach in three separate classrooms, none of which were "his," could not shake his excitement.

Many beginning teachers, especially those who are hired at "hiring fairs" in one part of the country for a school in a different part of the country, may come to the school situation in the same manner Travis did. Naïve about the community and hired late in the first quarter, Travis saw his hiring at Franklin as an adventure in many ways. It was not until he began driving halfway across the country that he began to consider where he was going and what he might find. However, thankful just to have a job, he figured that school would just "work out."

Unfortunately, many new teachers take that attitude. All new teachers, regardless of where they plan to teach, should research the school and its opportunities ahead of time. In addition, novices need to ask questions of those hiring them, especially if the interview takes place at a hiring fair. Although Travis expected to start teaching quickly, he was surprised to find that there was no set curriculum in place. In this situation, the hiring administrator could have made Travis's life easier by sharing information about the lack of specific curricular materials and which texts would be available for him to use. He could also have discussed the student population. Much of this conversation could have taken place in ten or fifteen minutes, but it certainly would have been an important allocation of time.

Support came to Travis in the form of his faculty mentor, Diane. Franklin's principal, obligated by the district's requirements for mentoring first- and second-year teachers, asked Diane if she would "talk with the new reading teacher, Travis . . . be a mentor." Specifically, he said, "Get a feel for how he is doing, and most important, see if he will make it, so we'll know if we should start looking for another person." Mr. Phelps, despite the suggestions made by the district, viewed the role of the mentor as more of an "informant" and less as a support for the novice teacher. Luckily for Travis, Diane, who had taught at Franklin for more than twenty years, had a different view of what it meant to mentor a beginning teacher in an urban setting.

Know Your Audience

Those who mentor first- or second-year teachers will most likely work with someone not much different than Travis—young, energetic, and idealistic. Most important, the mentee will most likely be a middle-class, white man or woman who grew up with a love for reading, writing, and language. Even if this is not exactly the case, the chances are high that these teachers will come from a different cultural background than the students they will be teaching. For many of these young, eager teachers, working in an urban setting may come as a bit of a shock to their system (and their envisioned pedagogies), even though most of them have graduated from education programs with formal instruction, informal discussions, and practicum or student teaching experiences that help them know what to expect in a variety of school situations. So why the lack of understanding?

Many beginning teachers think teaching in an urban site is a "humanitarian act." This misguided notion typically stems from the fact that the person grew up in a fairly privileged situation and feels he or she must "give back." These students tend to ignore the advice offered in university programs and/or during student teaching and take a job for which they may or may not be suited. Too often, they fail to do the research needed to understand the new community and are unwilling to change any of the pedagogical approaches they think necessary to teaching the content. They may well have forgotten Louise Rosenblatt's dictate, "I don't teach books; I teach students."

Other beginners may be teaching in urban sites because they can't leave the area because of a spouse or significant other or because they weren't able to obtain a job in the site of their choice. They also may feel that this job is a "temporary" situation on the way to a "real" job. Their attitude about the job and the particular school may well influence how they interact with students and colleagues alike.

Finally, some are simply like Travis: naïve but enthusiastic and willing to make the situation work no matter what. For these situations in particular, we'll continue to look at Diane and her mentoring of Travis.

Diane had worked with several student teachers during the last ten years of her career but had never had the opportunity to work as a mentor for a full-time teacher in her department before. Diane still found teaching fulfilling and rewarding, although she certainly had her share of moments when she questioned her career choice and the value of what she was doing. Diane grew up as part of the mainstream American culture, had a passion for language and literature, and entered teaching full of idealism and dreams of inspiring the minds of youths. Much like Travis, Diane found the experience of teaching in an urban setting much different from her imagined ideal situation. Yet Diane, without the help of a mentor, found intrinsic value and stimulation professionally, intellectually, and personally.

Because of her own successes, Diane embraced the role, as she saw much of herself in Travis and could easily identify with what he experienced during his first year of teaching.

Mentors can support beginning teachers' survival during the difficult and often disillusioning first year by

- Helping them understand the discrepancies between their idealistic expectations and the realities of the day-to-day job. University education programs tend to use the experts in their fields effectively to provide their students with both general approaches and specific ways to respond to content situations. However, they may not be as effective when providing future teachers with management plans that address a number of cultural or regional differences between students. In-the-building mentors are typically the best at helping beginning teachers make the shift between the theoretical knowledge and the practical know-how necessary for success in any school site.

- Helping novice teachers focus on the reasons why they became teachers in environments where morale is low or even nonexistent and teacher burnout is high. All school districts go through their highs and lows in terms of morale because of budget issues, political imperatives, and local situations. Veteran teachers learn the value of closing their classroom doors and teaching their students despite what goes on "outside." Novice teachers may need help understanding how to balance their love of content and students with the school and educational politics going on around them.

- Becoming an advocate for the beginning teacher. For example, Diana was aware that other districts could offer Travis more of the teaching he had initially imagined; therefore, she tried to get Franklin High School to be more responsive to his professional and intellectual interests. She urged the English department chair to schedule Travis for more intellectually demanding classes for his second year, and the following year, she pushed the administration to offer him more money to encourage his tenure at FHS. Advocacy of the type Diane offered may be difficult for most mentors to manage, especially during difficult budgeting times. However, the push for different types of classes was one that could be addressed as senior faculty thought Travis was ready. As we note throughout *Mentoring Beginning Teachers*, school districts may need to be creative in the manner in which they keep beginning teachers in the profession. Diane had a strong sense of that imperative.

Mentoring for Community Understanding

One of the first important steps Diane made with Travis was to introduce him to faculty members who also could serve as mentors. She talked with them privately and asked them to meet with Travis and talk with him about their experiences at Franklin. Diane selected faculty from virtually every department and every conceivable sociocultural background in the school, offering Travis a larger sense of community outside his content area.

Juarez Garcia became the most influential of these informal mentors. Juarez had attended Franklin as a student, and after graduation from a local university, moved back into the community. He and Travis immediately hit it off, and Juarez became an important resource for the younger teacher. For example, Travis had questions about violence, gang activity, and drug usage among his students and in the community. Having grown up in the community, Juarez offered insights the novice teacher could not receive from his university methods or theory courses. The older teacher discussed the clothing gang members wore, hand signals, and where the drug dealers hung out near and in the school. Juarez also spoke about many of the students' home lives, particularly the lives of immigrant students whose parents didn't speak English well or at all. Juarez not only raised Travis's awareness of some of the issues faced by his students, the community, and the school, but also provided an additional support system for the beginning teacher.

Juarez was able to provide an insider's view of Franklin High School that Diane could not have conveyed. Although there may not be a Juarez in all schools, a large number of teachers in urban schools grew up in similar settings and are familiar with life in that type of educational system. These mentors become especially helpful for beginners who lack familiarity with cultures other than their own.

Mentoring the "Extras"

Diane also found out that Travis had an interest in coaching. She encouraged him not to take on extra work his first year, but during the end of his first year at Franklin, she did help him make the connections with faculty members and administrators he needed to get involved in that facet of the school and community during his second year. Diane introduced Travis to Steve, one of the P.E. teachers as well as a three-sport coach. Travis and Steve hit it off immediately. The two sat down and talked about their love of sports and athletics. They swapped stories of their own involvement in sports during high school and college and talked about coaching issues. Travis was full of questions and Steve was happy to talk through them all, almost as if he were starved for the exchange and enthusiasm Travis's inquiry and interest ignited. Steve, like so many teachers, felt isolated in his professional work. Student, school, and community participation in athletics was low, and keeping athletes academically eligible was a weekly challenge. By the end of the conversation, Steve had provided Travis with a schedule for baseball season and an open door. Soon, Travis found himself spending more and more time working out in the weight room, swimming in the pool before school, and talking with Steve about coaching. Like Juarez, Steve provided Travis with another resource, another person to confide in and to work with. As a result, Travis coached boys' basketball during his second year at FHS and initiated a boys' lacrosse program at the school during his third.

Although we do not encourage first-year teachers to (willingly) take on extracurricular activities, there are times when they sign on, either as part of their actual teaching contract or because of a real desire to coach or sponsor a group of students in a particular activity. Mentors may, as in Diane's case, help beginning teachers find sensible mentoring within the coaching arena. In this sense, mentors need to look for coaches who value their teaching as highly as the sport or activity they sponsor so that the novice sees the importance of balancing teaching with the extra activity. They can also provide suggestions on how best to manage one's time during a coaching season. For example, suggestions on when to have assignments or projects due, how much homework to offer during tournament weeks, and so on can be helpful to the new coach or sponsor.

Mentoring to Lessen "Cultural Discontinuity"

The most obvious issue for Travis as a first-year teacher at FHS was the difference between his cultural background and that of his students. Growing up in a middle-class, largely Anglo suburb, Travis knew little of the realities of cultures other than his own. Diane, who had come from a similar background, had been teaching in the district for more than twenty years and understood that Travis needed help dealing with these tensions. At first, she suggested that they go out to lunch in the nearby Mexican restaurants where most of the staff and customers spoke Spanish; they also walked to the restaurants to get a feel for the community immediately surrounding the school. After some time, Diane suggested they drive to restaurants farther from the school to get familiar with the outer regions of the community in which the students lived. During these excursions, Diane would ask Travis about his students—their customs, language—and about his own background. Little by little she was helping him become familiar with not only the geographical space around the school but also the cultural "space" that existed between him and his students. Before long, their conversations turned to practical applications Travis could use in his classroom to capitalize on these differences rather than be intimidated by them. During one of their lunch conversations, Travis spoke passionately about an idea he had been thinking of trying in his classroom.

"My students don't speak or write English very well at all. When I hear them speak in Spanish or I let them write in Spanish, they seem to have few problems; in fact, I showed some of the papers written in Spanish to one of the interpreters you introduced me to, and she said the grammar and mechanics looked great in most of them. I'm wondering how I can use this to my—and their—advantage."

"What have you thought about?"

"Well, I'm thinking of somehow helping them see that what they already know about language is valuable and important and that now they have the opportunity to learn a 'new' language."

"Have you thought of having the students share their experiences with the intersection between their native language, which for most of our students is Spanish, and English?"

"I was thinking of having them do a project where they have to chart their use of language over the course of a day or two—when they use Spanish, when they use English. Then I'll have them think about what they need and want to know about English, based on their experiences, and go from there. I can develop lessons that pertain to what the students need and want to learn—whether it's related to reading, writing, speaking, watching a movie, anything."

"That sounds like a great idea," Diane replied with a smile.

Feelings of cultural discontinuity are typical with beginning teachers like Travis. When mentors can engage novices in discussions about how they will confront these tensions in their own classrooms, they provide a baseline for critical thinking on the topic. Diane's suggestions are helpful and insightful, but she is careful to use Travis's ideas as the beginning of the discussion.

However, there may also be times when the mentor needs to suggest specific approaches for understanding and dealing with feelings of cultural discontinuity. The mentor may

- Encourage the beginning teacher to talk with other newer teachers about their feelings of discontinuity and how they addressed them. This might occur at school in a one-on-one situation, or a mentor might invite a group of teachers to talk during an inservice or informal after-school get-together. It is important to encourage honesty and not make anyone feel bad because they had (have) these feelings at some point in their careers.

- Help the beginning teacher become more familiar with the community of which the school is a part. Diane and Travis's excursions to restaurants are a sensible beginning. The introduction to school sites that are part of the district—as discussed in the rural schools section of this chapter—can also help novice teachers better understand where students are coming from. Attending community festivities where beginning teachers might learn about the sociocultural background of their students, and maybe even see their students in a less formal atmosphere, may have excellent results.

- Support the new teacher in a variety of situations with parents and students. For example, when mentors can, they should sit in on parent/teacher conferences, especially if the new teacher does not speak the language in which a parent is most proficient.

Middle School Teaming Approaches

Middle schools in urban settings may be able to offer a different type of mentoring to beginning teachers. Because many middle schools have opted for a team approach to their teaching—combining English, math, social studies, and science teachers who then work with resource, art, music, physical education, and technology teachers as a group—student teachers and first-through-third-year teachers often find that instead of gaining one mentor, they gain at least three. Although we have previously discussed student teachers being negatively affected by the expectations of too many teachers, this chapter focuses on how the additional mentoring may help first- through third-year teachers become more comfortable in urban settings.

When we consider the concept of team mentors, we see the potential to create a strong mentor/beginning teacher relationship for many reasons. First, the members of the team commonly share a common prep period and lunch and have ample time to get to know each other and collaborate. Depending on the physical setup of the school, some teams even have common doors or offices, making it easier to get together for lunch or casual conversation between classes. In addition, because they share the same students, it may be easier for members of the team to model effective teaching, classroom management, and parent communication practices for beginning teachers. The teachers on a team can also meet and agree on consistent classroom management practices and brainstorm ways of creating a classroom and school environment conducive to learning.

The section on urban schools that features Travis pinpoints specific issues that many teachers new to urban teaching face. In the following section, so as not to repeat ourselves, we focus on a specific area where team mentoring can be an effective model for beginning teachers.

Mentoring for Community and Student Awareness

When Anne was hired to teach at a middle school in an inner-city neighborhood, she was assigned to a teaching team consisting of a language arts teacher, a social studies teacher, a science teacher, a math teacher, and an inclusion or ESL teacher or specialist. Anne was hired as a social studies teacher on the team, and her mentor, Jackie, was the language arts teacher. Jackie was very involved in the community and eager to meet Anne and work with her on the team. After their first meeting, Jackie suggested they get together for lunch that Saturday at a local deli near the school. Anne agreed, and meeting the owner of the popular lunch hangout was her introduction into the community. Jackie told Anne that by frequenting local restaurants, shops, and grocery stores, she often ran into parents and students and felt more a part of the community than she had when she first moved there. Even though Anne didn't live in the neighborhood, she followed Jackie's model by stopping at nearby stores on her way home rather than shopping in her suburban neighborhood.

She also attended her students' school-related athletics and extracurricular activities as well as any other performances or activities of which her students made her aware. Afterward, she would write a note to the student involved in the activity, commenting on something specific he or she had done. For example, to Rosie, who had been in a dinner theater performance of *The Philadelphia Story,* she wrote about how well she had taken on the East Coast accent necessary to make the character seem "real." Rosie's mother thanked Anne for writing the note when she ran into her daughter's teacher at the grocery store. Anne found that this kind of involvement helped her earn the respect of her students and their parents.

Francis, the team's math teacher, gave Anne a list of family services and student support services in the community, such as Big Brothers Big Sisters, the community food bank, a counseling center, a free health clinic, and a community center where kids could go after school. After checking out the various facilities, Anne asked the team if it would be appropriate to send a letter to parents letting them know about the various community offerings. They agreed, and it helped Anne feel that she was a viable member of the team, someone the others could count on just as she had come to count on them.

As shown in the cases above, both assigned and informal mentors can have immediate and long-lasting positive effects on beginning teachers. Jackie, as Anne's formal mentor, modeled a number of effective approaches for getting to know the community and the students through community activities. Her willingness to mentor both in and outside the school was important in helping Anne feel that she was not only part of the team but part of the community. Beginning teachers who are active in their schools are typically more likely to stay because they feel invested in their students' lives.

Francis's suggestions concerning community support services tapped into another important part of community life, especially in urban situations. Very often in rural locales, students, parents, and community members know each other from birth and, consciously or not, keep tabs on each other. Urban settings often do not have this measure in place, and support services can fill those voids. Again, helping Anne become more aware of the community and its services helps her as she works with students who may turn to her for help in times of need.

Mentoring the Daily Life of School

The school had recently implemented a gang awareness and prevention plan. The team discussed the warning signs during their meetings and brought up concerns about a number of students who might be more susceptible to gang activity. The five teachers also discussed problems they had faced in the past when they hadn't felt supported when they imposed various management techniques on their students. Those tensions, with both administrators and parents, had led to many students not feeling safe and protected at school. After much discussion, the teachers decided that all team members would follow the same classroom management program. With consistent rules and enforcement, they hoped that the students they worked with would feel like they were part of a community that shared common interests and goals. In addition, they planned and established integrated lessons and a plan for contacting parents weekly to give kudos to good students as well as to offer intervention for students who were struggling with anything from content knowledge to appropriate classroom behavior.

The approach used above has many factors working for it that makes it a good example of team mentoring. Because the group discusses and makes decisions as a team, they effectively model for Anne a number of lessons about planning, management, and working collegially and collaboratively. In essence, they are modeling professional behaviors that all beginning—and not so beginning—teachers need to learn and emulate.

Obviously one responsibility resulting from this plan would be for teachers to call parents more consistently. Like most beginning teachers, Anne was nervous about phoning parents, especially because she had not been expected to do this during student teaching. Anne's teammates helped her by role playing various types of parent phone calls and offering strategies for dealing with different types of parents. Baptista, the science teacher for the team, discussed challenges Anne would face in situations where parent communication might be difficult because of language barriers, socioeconomic issues, or a parent's distrust of the school system. Mentor teachers in urban schools should encourage rather than downplay the importance of interacting with parents, and should themselves have strong communication skills with parents that they can model for mentees.

Team members may also individually offer to sit in on meetings involving parents in the rare case that the team is not involved. Teams can also help beginning teachers get ready for parent night or open house by discussing the typical procedures connected with that activity and how they've welcomed parents to their individual rooms in the past.

Summary

We choose our first teaching placements for any number of reasons. One of our authors gratefully stayed in the school where she had been a student teacher because she figured she already understood the school, and it would prevent having to have a long-distance relationship with her boyfriend. One of our students chose to go back to the reservation where she had grown up because she thought she needed to give back to her community. Another beginning teacher chose to go to Alaska because of his desire for adventure and didn't even ask how large his classes would be or how many preps he could expect. Yet another chose a large urban setting because she knew she wanted to work with a culturally diverse student population.

We all move into those jobs with notions of what we want to accomplish. However, it is rare that any of us accomplish that in isolation, and for those of us moving into communities much different from the ones in which we were raised, successful mentoring can spell the difference between success and dis-appointment. Helping beginning teachers "get real" about their situations is important to their future success, and rural and urban sites must become even more effective in their approaches if they want to keep high-quality teachers in their classrooms.

Moving Across Buildings or Districts: Experienced Teachers in New Environments

There's a saying that you can't step into the same river twice: by the time you try to step back in again, some new water will have entered and some old water will have left. You can't read the same work twice either. By the second reading, you will have changed, just as the river did.

Alan C. Purves and Joseph A. Quattrini, *Creating the Literature Portfolio*

J ust as readers discover that books may change with a second reading, teachers often learn that new school districts or buildings create a new environment and additional transitions. Whereas some mentoring programs only address working with a student teacher or first-year teacher, other districts recognize the need to mentor experienced teachers new to a school building or district. As school districts are redesigned for multiage grading, consolidation, whole-grade sharing, or other configurations, teachers must often move to new environments, suddenly finding themselves as experienced teachers who are "new on the block."

This chapter highlights the importance of providing mentors not only to beginning teachers but also to those beginning at a new grade level, content area, or setting. In this chapter we provide mentors with a sense of the perplexity that "experienced beginning teachers" must feel in being partially knowledgeable but somewhat unaccustomed to the new system's proceedings. We provide strategies for mentors to welcome transfer teachers and help them feel at ease in the transition to their new surroundings.

Selecting Mentors for Transfer Teachers

Because transfer teachers bring experience and knowledge to their teaching, administrators should carefully select mentors and consider the following mentor qualities:

- a minimum of five years of teaching experience
- same grade level or curricular area
- close proximity in the building
- same age or older
- possibly same gender (See Chapter 3 for more specifics.)

Appreciating Strengths of Transfer Teachers

Unlike other beginning teachers, transfer teachers possess numerous people-related experiences. They bring a maturity based on past experiences and strengths from knowing school cultures and people interactions. They have the advantage of having already adapted to a school culture at least once.

Classroom management skills, parent communication, and lesson preparation abilities usually transfer fairly easily to a new situation. Occasionally, teachers discover that certain classroom management sayings or procedures are not appropriate for a higher or lower grade level, but most transfer teachers have little difficulty making these changes. Because transfer teachers bring experience and knowledge, they should feel valued by students, parents, colleagues, and administrators. Mentors can encourage transfer teachers to volunteer ideas, voice their opinions, and share practices that worked well in their former settings. For instance, they might summarize the advantages and disadvantages of practices such as outcome-based education, multiage classrooms, or block scheduling.

In the following sections, we provide suggestions for mentors to assist transfer teachers in adjusting more easily to their new environment.

Welcoming Transfer Teachers

Whether teachers are transferring within a district or to a new school system, most share similar needs such as discovering resources, learning school procedures, and adjusting to curricular differences. Because of this, transfer teachers often feel as if they are undergoing a first year again, and mentors can be important in supporting a smooth transition.

Specifically, mentors can help transfer teachers adjust to the new environment by giving a tour of the school and explaining daily procedures. Changes such as computerized attendance and/or grades may seem minute, but they may be somewhat disconcerting to a transfer teacher.

School districts should provide an introductory welcoming notebook to help simplify the procedures followed by the school's teachers, principal, and students. This notebook might include some or all of the following:

- school district mission and vision statements
- school goals and philosophy
- school lore such as school colors, mascot, song lyrics, and traditions
- school calendar
- building schedule listing all teachers, rooms, and classes
- map of the building
- attendance and discipline forms
- forms for supplies or repairs, teacher-leave days, or parental permission
- words or acronyms specific to the building or school district (for example, terms for special education classes and lockdowns)

Mentors can guide transfer teachers through this welcoming notebook, checking for questions or differences from a former system. Schools often have their own language and acronyms for special education, talented and gifted programs, or other curricular areas. Including a page about these specialized areas can be helpful, or mentors can clarify language issues.

Teachers Moving from Other Districts

Although transfer teachers moving from other districts may already possess classroom management and planning skills, these educators will need assistance in the following areas:

- curriculum standards, benchmarks, and assessments
- knowledge of what is taught in previous and later grades or courses
- curriculum resource materials
- knowledge of the community (such as businesses)
- knowledge of student populations (such as ethnic diversity and socioeconomic status)
- information about the school district, its policies (such as leave forms) and its traditions (such as homecoming)
- policies and practices for disciplinary issues
- information on parent/teacher conferences, open houses, and other types of parent communication
- practices for special-needs students (special education, gifted and talented, and second-language learners) such as referral forms

Mentors can play an important role in helping teachers new to the district become acclimated by assisting with curricular changes, encouraging the teacher's voice in faculty discussions, or helping with multiple changes such as working with parents or decreasing emotional stress.

Assisting with Curricular Changes

Many transfer teachers find it hard to let go of favorite curricular units. They often must forgo a known success and perhaps exchange it for a topic of lesser interest. In the following scenario, the mentor leads the transfer teacher into new ways of viewing former materials or ideas:

"Jo Ellen, do you have any questions about the curriculum?"

"Well, I understand what I'm supposed to teach and when I can include some of my own choices. I'm just disappointed that I can't teach my mythology unit. I've collected lots of multicultural stories from around the world, but it sounds like that's being taught in seventh grade rather than eighth grade."

"That's too bad. Would you feel comfortable sharing your materials with the seventh-grade teachers or working in a couple of days of review?"

"That's a good idea. I could check with the seventh-grade team. If not, maybe I could include Native American myths after a Native American short story or poem. Maybe I could use the African myths on a day between units."

Mentors can offer options, such as in the above example, of sharing the unit with others or breaking it into mini-lessons for review or expansion. Most important, though, they must realize that this issue is often more about emotion than content. The transfer teacher may feel comfortable and secure with the familiar and find it difficult to be a risk-taker, to explore new ideas. Mentors can listen attentively, ask about successful past transitions or adjustments, confirm the individual's value, and explore the teacher's tentativeness toward a new curricular area. Finally, mentors can talk about the transfer teacher's opportunity to learn new concepts and reinvigorate his or her teaching, aspects that lie at the heart of moving to a new building or district.

Encouraging a Teacher's Voice

One way a mentor can help a transfer teacher feel a part of a new community is to encourage the individual to voice opinions. In the following scenario, Phyllis encourages Ramon to discuss his feelings about adjusting to a new school team:

"Ramon, how are things going?"

"Well, I've made it through the first few months, so I've gotten used to most of the changes."

"What seems to be going well?"

"I really like the students and the faculty. It's been a lot of work, but that seems to be going OK."

"What concerns do you have?"

"Oh, nothing really important. I just didn't realize how many changes I would have to make. It's also been hard to move to the bottom rung of the ladder."

"What do you mean?"

"I had forgotten how long it takes to earn respect."

"Don't you feel accepted?"

"Sure, everyone has been really friendly, but my team and the rest of the faculty seem to have always done things a certain way. I don't feel very comfortable making suggestions, and when I do, they usually decide to keep doing things the same way. I can understand that, but it's kind of frustrating."

If transfer teachers have been leaders in a previous school, they may be surprised if their suggestions don't receive the same degree of respect in a new school system. The transfer teacher may feel silenced or ignored. Because respect must be gradually earned, transfer teachers may feel like they should reserve their comments for topics about which they are the most knowledgeable. Others, such as grade-level partners or team members, may be comfortable in their old patterns and may not be sensitive to the needs of the transfer teacher. All teachers should be responsible for nurturing their colleagues. Mentors, as well as administrators, can model helping transfer teachers find a voice by asking the transfer teacher, "Do you have any ideas or suggestions?" or "Did your previous school have a good way of handling this situation?" If mentors invite the transfer teacher to share ideas in team or building meetings or even in hallway or faculty lounge discussions, other colleagues may follow the lead in being open to the new teacher's ideas.

Sometimes the transfer teacher brings skills and strengths that threaten others in the building. An enthusiastic transfer teacher may make a burned-out teacher feel jealous when she hears a student say, "I like Mrs. Johnson's class." In other instances, a transfer teacher may repetitively ask "Why?," which can be misconstrued as criticism rather than needing information. Even though educators often dislike admitting it, much of school life involves the politics of working with colleagues and administrators. Mentors may need to help their teams adjust to a new member, gently reminding them that being open-minded is part of being professional. Similarly, mentors will probably need to help transfer teachers adjust to this political environment.

Addressing Differences in Student Populations

Mentors can also assist transfer teachers in understanding the specific student population. In the following scenario, Lana explains to Carolyn the adjustments she has had to make in moving from a low to a high socioeconomic district:

Lana, a second-grade teacher for fifteen years in a low-income school district, suddenly found herself—because of her husband's job transfer—with a new second-grade position in a university town. Lana had impressed the interview committee with her adaptations for students from a nonliteracy home environment. However, when she arrived at McElfry Elementary, she felt as if she were in a future time zone. Her spacious classroom included a desk phone, a mini-computer lab, and a VCR/TV dangling from the ceiling. Her new learning process included using computerized attendance and grading, as well as the district's Web page to obtain benchmarks and professional-leave forms. Although she had continually tried to update her technological skills, she now felt antiquated.

Lana glanced at her familiar bulletin boards and files of materials. Feeling once again secure in the world of second graders, she immersed herself in preparations. The second-grade team had told her that they started the year with units on community helpers, bicycle safety, and pet care, so she pulled out her familiar, previously successful units. Within only a few days, though, Lana found herself floundering. Her new second-grade class had raced through much of her first three-week unit, and she had to add writing activities and supply more reading resources. She now realized that she needed to upgrade all of her units to meet her students' needs. Although she had expected some adjustments to a new school, she was not prepared to revise her entire curriculum.

Carolyn, Lana's mentor, felt honored when her principal asked her to mentor Lana. Having been present at Lana's interview and having read all her glowing recommendations, she thought the mentoring situation could be reciprocal, that she could learn as much from Lana as Lana could from her. During the before-school preparation, she had been delighted by Lana's colorful, active-learning classroom environment. During the first days of school, Lana smiled whenever Carolyn asked, "How did it go today?"

On Friday, though, when Lana returned from bus duty, she collapsed into her teacher chair. Across the hall, Carolyn noted Lana's weariness, entered the room, and empathized, "Wow, you look exhausted. The first week takes its toll, doesn't it?"

"Oh, I didn't think it would be this hard."

"It sounded like things went well this week. What's wrong?"

"The kids here are so far ahead of the ones at my other school."

Carolyn laughed. "And that's a problem?"

Lana grinned. "I guess I should appreciate the literate environment these kids have had. Their parents have read them books and taken them to museums and historical sites. Several of my second graders have traveled to other countries. It's amazing."

"How could we have better prepared you for this?"

"I guess I would have liked to have known more about the student population during the inservices. I'd like to have known more about my students before the first day of school."

"Thanks. I'll mention that to our mentor coordinator, so she can include it in future inservices. But what's the problem right now?"

"I feel out of my league. These kids are zooming through all of my materials. I'm going to have to make big changes to my units."

"How about if we do it together? It's time for me to revamp my units. I bet Darlene would like to join us, too. Shall we do it?"

"That sounds good," Lana admitted.

In this scenario, Lana illustrates the need for schools to provide an analysis of the student population before the school year. Whereas Lana was adapting to a higher socioeconomic population, the situation could be reversed, with the transfer teacher discovering that her materials are too advanced for her new students. Ways to acclimate the new transfer teacher include the following:

- provide details of the district's population (such as cultural heritages and socioeconomic background)

- invite teachers hired before the end of a term to observe classes

- give the transfer teacher a tour of area homes and businesses and industries to obtain a sense of the environment (Commuting teachers often drive on main highways or streets and do not receive an overview of the community.)

- work with the transfer teacher to analyze class abilities and match unit plans

Meeting the needs of the audience is the key to good teaching. Even though Lana felt dismayed that she would have to devote more time and energy to unit development, Carolyn's suggestion for a team approach made the upcoming struggle seem much more manageable, perhaps even enjoyable.

Understanding the Culture of the Community

Understanding the student population can help transfer teachers recognize community expectations. Because Lana didn't have an accurate picture of the students, she also was surprised by parental expectations:

McElfry's open house was held during the fourth week of school. Many of her students' parents were either doctoral students or university professors. They not only wanted to hear about their child's performance, but they questioned her about her theoretical stance, pedagogical practices, curricular reform, and multiple assessments. As the last parents left, she felt emotionally drained.

"How did it go?" Carolyn asked as Lana kicked off the heels she had donned for the open house.

"OK, I guess," Lana acknowledged. "But I'm used to having parents ask me, 'Is Robert sassing you? If he is, he'll hear about it at home.' Tonight I was asked about phonemic awareness, math manipulatives, and science labs. These parents have really high expectations for their children."

"You're right. It took a while for me to adjust to the expectations, too. If a student doesn't do well, we immediately hear from the parents."

"I guess that's good, but it almost feels like I'm constantly having someone looking over my shoulder. I guess I should just remind myself that having parents ask for accountability is a positive thing."

Experienced teachers often feel a sense of displacement when a typical situation, such as parent/teacher conferences, becomes atypical. Mentors can help transfer teachers see the positive aspects of the new environment. In this situation, Carolyn mentored Lana by sharing her own experience, which perhaps helped her feel less isolated. Other ways a mentor might support a transfer teacher include discussing the community before the school year or going beyond empathy ("It happened to me, too") to question the transfer teacher about the parent-teacher conference. For instance, before the conferences Carolyn might have asked, "What do you think will be typical parental expectations of you and the students?" In discussing the community, Carolyn can help Lana obtain a whole picture of her surroundings.

Lowering Stress Levels

Like anyone else moving to a new community, Linda experienced professional and personal stress in leaving one community and becoming acquainted with a new one.

"How are things on the home front?" asked Melanie, popping into Linda's room three weeks into the school year.

"Oh, as good as can be expected, I guess. I feel only half moved in. I still have boxes to unpack, we haven't hung pictures yet, and we've been living off pizza deliveries and take-home Chinese until I get my school life under control."

"It sounds like you've been doing a lot."

Linda laughed. "I think I've been trying to be Superwoman, and it isn't working. I've been unpacking, writing thank-you notes from the going-away party, getting things ready here in the classroom, and spending time with my own kids."

"How are they adjusting?"

"Um, so-so. They're at difficult ages for a move. They miss their old friends, and they haven't gotten new friends yet."

"How about if I host a second-grade-team potluck at my house on Friday night? My husband likes to barbecue, so we could grill hot dogs and hamburgers. It wouldn't be anything fancy, just a fun time together. Several of us have kids, and they could play volleyball in our backyard. What do you think?"

"Great. We'd love to get out of the house and away from the unpacking for a night."

Although we often think about the emotional adjustments that beginning teachers make from college life to the K–12 school system, we rarely consider the adjustment that transfer teachers also make both emotionally and socially. Mentors do not have to make overtures of barbecues, as Melanie did, but talking about the emotional changes may be helpful. A mentor can invite personal conversations and serve as a listener, share a list of community resources such as the YMCA and library, suggest youth organizations such as the Scouts, and/or ask for questions about negotiating a new community. Helping with personal adjustments does not need to be a requirement of mentoring, but many new teachers appreciate this personal touch.

Teachers Moving Within the District

Teachers who have already been a part of the school system are familiar with the district and its policies; however, they may face challenges such as the following:

- different school building policies
- new grade or subject areas
- unfamiliar curricular units or texts
- changes in parent/teacher conferences, open houses, or grading
- contrasts in expectations and leadership styles of department chairs or administrators

- varying traditions
- differences in building politics

As noted previously, probably the greatest change for the transfer teacher may be changes in how the curriculum is presented to students. Although it is important for all beginning teachers to have a mentor at the same grade level or curricular area, it is even more crucial for teachers transferring from one building to another. Mentors need to explain the standards and benchmarks for the new subject or grade level and assist with curricular resources. Like other transfer teachers, the individual who is transferring from another building may feel dismayed at not teaching certain areas and uncomfortable with new curricular topics.

The welcoming notebook for this teacher should include materials related to the specific building. Once again, this educator may feel uncomfortable speaking at faculty meetings, so mentors can encourage the transfer teacher's contributions.

Recognizing Differences in Students

Sometimes teachers transferring from another building must adjust to different curricular areas or different ages of students. In the following scenario, notice Glenn's use of questioning to help Brandon consider new ways of thinking about his teaching:

Brandon looked at Glenn, his mentor. "The hardest adjustment I'm having to make in moving from middle school social studies to high school history is figuring out appropriate expectations. If you remember, I didn't want to move to high school. I didn't have a choice, so I'm not sure how much of this is not being aware and how much is not being willing to make the move. However, I decided I have to focus on the current situation and make the best of it."

"Great. It sounds like you've overcome the first hurdle. Are there any problems you'd like to discuss?"

"Well, I know I'm not asking deep enough questions, but then I overcompensated by asking questions that were too tough and didn't get any response."

Glenn smiled. "So how can you find the right balance?"

"I don't know. I guess I'll have to keep experimenting."

"Have you tried writing down the questions?"

"No. I guess after class I could mark the ones that receive the most student response or the most amount of critical thinking."

"That sounds good. Any other changes you've noticed?"

"Uh-huh. The first test I made was too easy, and the second test was too hard. I have the same problem in giving directions—I either over- or under-do it."

"Would you like me to look over the assessments you give?"

"Sure, would you?"

As this conversation reveals, a transfer teacher may feel frustrated in meeting the needs of students from a different grade level. Mentors can help transfer teachers adapt to the new age group by asking the transfer teacher to describe successes, analyze problem areas, determine possible changes, assess the pros and cons of the changes, and develop ways to assess progress.

Brandon's situation also shows the effect of a forced move. If the transfer change is an administrative directive rather than a voluntary request, the adjustment may be more profound. In cases like this one, Glenn, as mentor, needs to help Brandon feel like part of a new community as well as help him with the practical aspects of teaching. He may also need to be a listener and questioner, helping Brandon unearth some of the resentment he may feel in making what he initially viewed as an unwelcome change. Mentoring often serves as a bridge connecting the emotional and curricular aspects of teaching.

Adjusting to Differences in Programs

Teachers transferring within the school system usually experience a much easier and quicker adjustment than teachers new to the district. However, teachers transferring across buildings often expect few changes and are surprised at the differences in building cultures and programming.

After ten years of teaching first grade at Cline Elementary, LeTyshia asked for a transfer to Washington Elementary so she could have a shorter commute. She felt at ease working with emerging readers in first grade, but she noted numerous changes she hadn't expected.

"I'm still getting used to the system here," LeTyshia told her mentor, Joan.

"What's different?" Joan asked.

"Here the special education and the talented and gifted students are mainstreamed instead of pulled out. I'm still getting used to having other teachers assist me in the classroom."

"I guess that would be different. What else?"

"I didn't think there would be so many variables since we have the same district curriculum and benchmarks. However, this building has more emphasis on reading with Read a Million Minutes and DEAR [Drop Everything and Read]. Also the fourth graders are reading buddies for my first graders. This building seems to have more celebrations such as One Hundred Week in finding different ways to count to 100. There's more parent involvement, too, and a Parent University Night for parents to learn how to help their children at home. All of these programs are great. It's just taking a while for me to get used to all these new changes."

"I didn't realize that two buildings in the same system would be so different. How can I help you with these changes?"

"Keep telling me what's coming up. Keep asking me if I'm familiar with this or that program. Keep me informed—I don't like surprises!"

"OK, that sounds easy enough."

Many times transfer teachers have taught in only one setting and expect procedures to be universal. Mentors can assist transfer teachers by explaining specific programs. Notice Joan's positive approach to LeTyshia's dilemma: "How can I help you with these changes?" Even though she didn't foresee the problems, Joan is ready to assist LeTyshia and to learn from the situation. Preparing a list of school programs with a short description and providing a school calendar that lists these activities can help transfer teachers like LeTyshia feel part of rather than distanced from the school community.

Summary

Transfer teachers bring many talents with them to their new teaching position. Classroom management, unit planning, and parent communication skills usually transfer easily from one district or one building to another. These educators possess experience as well as new perspectives to enrich the school system.

Mentoring transfer teachers may be different from mentoring new teachers. The mentor's role in such cases calls for sensitivity and thought regarding possible obstacles. The mentor needs to invite the transfer teacher to share successes, questions, and problems. Showing respect for a transfer teacher's experiences can help the teacher feel respected and valued. Because a transfer teacher may struggle with different school dynamics and culture, the mentor may need to describe the student population and community expectations as well as help the transfer teacher negotiate and adjust to a new environment. If the mentor adopts a positive attitude, the transfer teacher often reflects a similar perspective. By appreciating their talents while being conscious of changes, mentors can help transfer teachers adapt more readily to a new school culture.

Mentoring the Teacher Teaching At-Risk Students

Eric stood in the doorway a minute before entering his classroom. Fifteen students today. Yesterday, there had been eight. Clay was back today, his newly cut Mohawk a neon green. Marcy was smiling, gazing out the window, but Eric couldn't help but notice that she was wearing a turtleneck in the eighty-five-degree heat. Jack and Tony just looked annoyed. Oh, and there was a new girl sitting in the second row who didn't look nearly nervous enough. He glanced at the memo from the principal. Josie Connock, kicked out of K. Stacy High School for starting a number of fights with other girls in her class. Eric stood a second longer, forced a smile to his face, and walked through the door.

Fifty minutes later, the smile was gone and Eric stood in the doorway of his colleague Juan's classroom. "I'm not sure how much more of this I can take," Eric said. "Nothing prepared me for this. I mean, I learned about management methods in one of my classes, but not a single one of them works with this group."

"It's tough, I know," Juan said reassuringly, "when you've got kids who have already been bounced out of two or three schools, who are truant more often than not, who just don't see the value of what you're teaching. But you can't give up on them, and you can't give up on yourself. Why don't we talk through some approaches that you haven't tried yet? They may sound unorthodox, but I think you'll find them pretty helpful as you deal with the Jacks and Tonys and Marcys in your classroom."

Eric is one of the growing number of beginning educators teaching in alternative high schools around the country. His conversation with Juan is a necessary one when considering how schools can best keep dedicated teachers working with those students labeled "at-risk." For the purposes of this chapter, we use a definition for at-risk students and alternative schools from Gay Knutson of Carroll College (2002).

> *At-risk students are described as discouraged learners, those who for whatever reason do not achieve in the standard high school program. Poor attendance, habitual truancy, academic lags, and teenage parenthood—these are the causes of what the federal definition specifies as school drop-outs, from 9th to 12th grade. Over 25 percent of American youth fit that description.*
>
> *The term alternative education was originally construed as an umbrella term covering a range of options in schooling. Presently its meaning has evolved into an understanding of programming for at-risk youth; those who are likely to not finish high school . . . alternative schools for at-risk students have been in existence for several years. Alternative high schools have grown nationally in both quality and number. These schools for both existing and potential drop-outs rely heavily on forming learning communities where both teacher and learner are empowered. Innovation and flexibility are usual practice in alternative high schools. (horizon.unc.edu/projects/HSJ/Knutson.asp)*

The last ten to fifteen years have seen a serious growth in the number of programs implemented by schools and communities to help at-risk students. If you plug "at-risk students" into the search engine on your Web browser, you will likely find anywhere from 50,000 to 300,000 sites that have something to do with the definition of, or programs and approaches to, working with at-risk students. However, what you won't discover is how to mentor the teachers who work with those students. In this chapter, we further refine our definition of at-risk students and alternative educational settings, talk with a number of teachers who work with at-risk students, and discuss a number of issues connected to mentoring new teachers hired to work with them. The teachers interviewed for this chapter discuss what they wish they had known before they became teachers of at-risk students or what they experienced those first weeks on the job. They share what they do to mentor the new teachers with whom they work. Finally, they offer advice to administrators and to universities about what they can do to better prepare and support teachers who want to work with at-risk students.

Defining the "At-Risk Student" and the "Alternative" Middle/High School

Ask a random group of people what comes to mind when you say the term *at-risk students* and most of them will probably tell you these are "kids who have gotten kicked out of high school or don't fit in for some reason or another." Ask them to talk about an *alternative school* and, depending on the state in which they live, they will offer their ideas on charter schools, magnet schools, or schools for kids who are down to their last chance at completing an education without resorting to a GED.

We asked a group of teachers who are teaching in alternative middle and high schools what they considered to be the main characteristics of alternative schools for at-risk students. The following were the most often shared. Alternative schools

- take the students who don't fit in for any number of reasons in the regular middle or high school;

- have administrators and teachers who are more aware of the need to respond to diversity issues that may affect student learning;

- understand the need for smaller classes and more student-to-student interactions as well as effective teacher-to-student relationships to foster a community of learners;

- are more flexible in terms of classroom setup, time issues, and curriculum. They can be more responsive to individual needs and challenge them accordingly. This, in turn, allows teachers to make the curriculum more relevant to students;

- use different types of management, usually more flexible approaches to keep students coming to school;

- give some students and families another option for providing the student with the education he or she needs. They accept the reality that many of these kids have full-time jobs because they must have the income. These schools may provide an environment in which to "start over";

- offer the vocational tracks that seem to have disappeared from traditional schools;

- provide a service-learning component to help students understand that they're part of a community and that the members of that community can learn from each other.

Using these characteristics as a backdrop for this chapter, let's look further at what mentors who have spent a number of years teaching in alternative schools may do to help new colleagues.

Insights from "the Front Lines"

And the most important thing is this: you have to really love teaching and feel like you're good at it before you move into an alternative school situation. I honestly don't think that first- and second-year teachers can be successful in an alternative situation. And if you don't absolutely love teaching, alternative school experiences can drive you away from the profession.
    Frank, veteran teacher

The Work of the Mentor

When I was asked to mentor someone new to our building, my first words to him were, "You will look back on this first week and be amazed at how good you feel about what you've accomplished . . . because you'll also know how hard you've worked this week to make the successes, however small they may be, happen."
    Frank

Mentoring a colleague new to the whole alternative high school situation is, in many ways, similar to any mentoring one might be asked to do. However, teachers mentoring in alternative high schools do suggest some necessary deviations from the norm. In the following section, Frank, Sylvia, and Tom, veteran teachers and strong mentors, share some pointers they have picked up over the years.

Realistic Expectations

"One of the most important things I share with new teachers to our program," said Frank, "is that miracles are hard to come by in this school. I think there is probably too high a percentage of teachers who come to this school thinking that they're going to 'save' someone. Maybe they will, but I consider myself pretty successful when I see kids making those small, positive gains—getting work in on time, taking some pride in a project they produce for class, not striking out when they're frustrated. These are realistic expectations for our students. I think that we foster these gains through the variety of choices we make as teachers and through those we can help our students make."

When asked how he would help a new teacher to the alternative school setting understand "realistic expectations," Frank shared the following story:

A few years ago we had a young teacher, Pete, who came to us thinking that he could best get through to kids by "speaking their language." Pete was young, hip by his own definition, and culturally aware, even though he wasn't from a minority group represented in our school. When I went in to observe him, he was trying to have a discussion with them, but they were tuning him out and laughing at him when he used "their" slang. Pete was genuinely frustrated at the end of the class, and when we talked, he told me that the kids weren't responding to him the way he had imagined they would.

"What did you expect?" I asked Pete.

Pete said he thought many kids became alienated in traditional high schools because teachers didn't understand their cultural identity: their language, their clothes, their worldview. Although I agreed with some of his assessment, I questioned his perception that they would feel more comfortable if he looked and acted like them. In my experience, kids aren't looking for a new best friend in their teacher; I believe this whether one is teaching in a traditional or alternative high school. What they really need are teachers they can look to for guidance and role modeling, teachers who are willing to spend more time listening to their problems and complaints about their situations, or their failure to learn, whatever it may be. And we do have more of an opportunity to do that in our school because we typically have fewer students per class per day.

I talked to Pete about helping students come to terms with why they are in our school. Some really don't want to be here and just want to quit school altogether; others are frustrated that they can't finish quickly enough to "get on with their lives." A few of the kids who are here are way too comfortable with our setup and don't want to put themselves back into the traditional school setting where they face more pressure concerning grades, conforming to expectations. We do a great deal of individualizing our instruction, so I suggested that Pete do more individual projects that would allow him to work at a different level with students and give them the opportunity to see an activity through from beginning to end. I believe this is a really important factor in our work with kids, this opportunity to succeed and to master their situations in a proactive manner. I'd say again, these are reasonable expectations for our students because they reflect what the kids will need out in the world.

In this situation, Frank talks to Pete about ways to think through his own expectations to provide realistic goals for students. It is important for teachers new to an alternative program to repeatedly consider their own perceptions to confirm whether or not they are accurate. A mentor like Frank can be especially helpful because he has already experienced many of the same situations and perceptions.

Understanding the Students

Sylvia, a veteran teacher who actually began her career in an alternative high school, underscores the "absolute necessity" of a formal mentoring program for teachers new to the alternative school because of student issues:

I think that it is especially important that faculty take care of each other. This is one school situation where you're not going to get much from the kids in terms of "positive strokes" for what you're doing for them. These kids get in your face; you have to learn not to take it personally. A mentor familiar with this situation can be a great help in the "desensitizing" process. For example, I was working with a young teacher a few years ago who had said all the right things when we interviewed her. However, when she was actually in the classroom situation, she didn't have the flexibility necessary to make it in the alternative setting, and she got really upset when she became involved in direct verbal confrontations and the students wouldn't back down. I think the hardest thing for new teachers to this kind of system is realizing that somewhere along the line, many of these kids lost their ability to trust. A large number of them really don't have empathy for others' feelings, either. And that makes the teacher's job harder, because she has to constantly earn and re-earn the students' respect and trust. They have short attention spans and very long memories, especially when the teacher "screws up." In all fairness, they do forgive . . . but probably only once. So the teacher's job becomes that much harder; we can make a mistake, but we better make that mistake only once or the trust is gone.

Sylvia's comments are important in helping teachers new to this setting understand where students may be "coming from." Often, home situations are the initial factors in explaining why some adolescents distrust adults. A mentor can clarify the origin of students' attitudes as well as explain more effectively why student comments cannot be taken as personal attacks on a teacher's authority.

Mentoring and Teaming

Tyler, who teaches in a "reentry program" (a program for students who have been suspended or expelled from one of the city high schools) notes that he had no expectations beyond wanting to "help these kids" before he began teaching in the alternative high school. Tyler had student-taught in a multi-ethnic middle school with a structured curriculum and had faced what he considered the typical management issues new educators face.

I had kids who couldn't keep their mouths shut, who wanted negative attention, who didn't get their homework done. My cooperating teacher was really solid about how to handle these situations, so I left student teaching feeling like I could handle students. However, we didn't have huge truancy problems, and we certainly weren't dealing with a lot of kids doing drugs or drinking. So my first day here was a shock, even though I've always said I wanted to work with kids who needed more one-on-one time, more patience. To be honest, if it hadn't been for Tom, the guy I team-teach with, I wouldn't have made it through the first month because we weren't assigned any mentors. Daily I would approach him, tell him a situation, how I handled it, and ask him how he would handle it. He would laugh at me, encourage me, and give me different things to consider. He was my mentor, all day, every day.

In discussing why his relationship with Tom worked, Tyler brought up some of the same issues any beginning teacher might. Tom helped Tyler consider various approaches toward classroom management, curricular issues, and student/teacher interactions. However, by necessity, Tom's instruction went beyond what a mentor in a traditional school might be asked to provide; Tom's experience, as well as the manner in which he modeled for Tyler how to reach alternative students, were instrumental in fostering Tyler's success. Tyler noted:

The biggest way that Tom has helped me has been the constant interaction. For a lot of the first year, we worked together, and I was able to see him in action on a regular basis. Also, he didn't just tell me what he thought would work, he modeled it. Every day I got to see him model what worked with different kids and I would think, "Oh, that's how I could deal with this or that situation." Working with at-risk youth, I needed the constant modeling because situations would arise many times an hour. I think in other classes the same problems wouldn't arise with the same intensity or frequency and one could simply save questions for a weekly mentor meeting. This type of educational situation provides a more intense setting, and we have problems that need to be addressed quickly.

Tom concurred with Tyler, adding that

Modeling is the key. And I think that it's just a good habit to get into, mentors modeling for those they mentor just as they model appropriate behaviors and approaches for students. I know that watching and listening to others is important in my growth, and I would argue that it's the same for beginning teachers and students, whether they are in an alternative situation or not. But it may be even more significant for our kids because they may not be getting enough appropriate modeling at home or among their peers. So I see the mentoring not simply benefiting junior colleagues but also getting those of us who mentor often to internalize the need to model, model, model. The patience, the flexibility, the problem-solving abilities they see in my work with Tyler affects their choices for behavior.

Tom and Tyler, and mentor and mentored, underscore why collegial relationships benefit from mentoring. Not only was Tyler positively influenced by Tom's support, but their students were also affected by their modeling of appropriate behaviors. Team teachers can give each other momentary relief from the pressures that often build up in the alternative classroom, an important factor in helping students see productive ways of controlling and using their emotions.

The Concerns of the Mentored

The Downside of Teaming and Mentoring

Although teaming and mentoring at the same time worked well for Tyler and Tom, other teachers with whom we talked had a different view of teaming situations.

"I like teaming, but I don't recommend having your mentor be your partner," said Claire, a veteran teacher who was just finishing her first year in an at-risk school. "Maybe the problem is that my partner, Ben, and I knew each other from teaching in the same building in the traditional system a few years ago, so we know each other's history. In addition, we have very different styles of teaching, and that has caused its own problems. Add to that the fact that we must plan together as an interdisciplinary team. Add to that that he has been here two years longer than I have. Add to that that our school district has a formal mentoring program and because Ben has served as a mentor to others in the past, the principal here decided that that automatically made Ben my mentor. And the sum is a big problem for me because I don't feel like I can go to Ben with honest concerns because he'll be judging me and telling me to do it his way. I really think that I would be better off with a mentor from outside our building who has had some experience working in the at-risk site. Because with Ben . . . well, let me put it this way: If we're not arguing over some 'turf' issue, then we're arguing over how best to deal with a student who has set us up like parents, you know, the mom (me) said I could, so Dad (Ben) should, too. It wears on me. I can't imagine coming back next year unless some things change. And I feel bad about that, because I think I could do well in this environment."

In a situation like Claire's, we see obvious reasons why the administrator should be playing a more active role in the professional life of his teachers. Although many teachers might welcome working with someone with whom they have positive history, the relationship between Ben and Claire does not seem to lend itself to that. In addition, any mentoring situation where one member of the team does not feel that she can be honest virtually negates any chance that discussions between the two will be healthy. This is certainly a case that demands a switch, and Claire needs to request a different mentor from her principal.

Knowledge of Student Behaviors

Another issue that many teachers brought up concerned the lack of information about the attitudes and behaviors of students in the alternative setting. Olivia, a recent addition to the faculty at the alternative site on her campus, noted

---

"I don't know if it's just my school, but I wasn't prepared for them to 'get in my face' the way they did. That's not to say I didn't expect them to have attitude, because I expected a certain macho from my male students, an assertiveness, a 'tough' atti-tude from the students. But I got no heads-up from my principal during the inter-view; in fact, he said they were quite well behaved, considering the alternative situation. Well, suffice it to say that I didn't expect them to be so vocal about every-thing, and, the first time I had a student tell me to 'F--k off, you lousy b---h' in front of the whole class, I almost walked out of the room. It took everything I had to stand there, and some kids told me later they saw me shaking and were sure I would start crying. But I just knew that if I left the room, I wouldn't be able to come back. I han-dled the situation, but it would have been nice to have been warned."

Many teachers have certain expectations about the rigor of working with at-risk students, but mentors need to be honest about issues of student popu-lation, potential violence, and expected support. "Forewarned is forearmed," said Frank, "and while we have virtually no incidents of violent behavior in our school, we do have enough talk about it that I plan accordingly to ensure that certain kids won't be asked to work together."

Curriculum and Time on Task Issues

Tyler also shared some of his comments about the curriculum:

The most difficult aspect for me, after the in-your-face issue, has been the preparing-for-student-learning issue. Specifically, I've had to learn to make adjustments based on the amount of time I have most of my students, the fact that the class is constantly changing in terms of who shows up, and how to plan a curriculum that benefits the "been-heres" as well as the latecomers. I get new students every week; mature stu-dents move on every ten weeks. That makes it extremely difficult to do many of the ideal things I always dreamed of, like having students come up with rules that they have to work by or creating four-week-long projects. The one ideal thing I can do, though, is individualize my instruction. I can really talk with my students about what they need or what seems relevant to them in their life. Of course, the problem with that is that I lack a lot of the resources I could really use to teach—for example, basic grammar in a more creative way, or a wider choice of literature. A "real" English department, rather than just me, would be a bonus in that regard.

However, I would say that I have learned to be more creative. For example, we just did a play of the courtroom scene in *To Kill a Mockingbird*. All the students (including the jury) dressed up nicely and we acted it out through reading the parts we'd written earlier. It was awesome. The only thing we changed was that Tom Robinson was white and all the others (lawyers, jury, Ewells, judge, etc.) were black. We changed the "n" word to *cracker.* We had a good time.

Tyler's comments are important in terms of the role of the curriculum. Although most of our alternative school teachers prided themselves on offering differentiated instruction, many mourned the lack of content-area co-planning. Larger school districts may be able to accommodate content-area planning, but smaller districts, which often hire only one teacher in each content area, can only offer the suggestion to share curricular materials with another local school. Although that can help in certain situations, it may not alleviate problems connected with lack of supplies and materials, much less the collegial necessity of having other content mentors.

Training and Support

Many of the alternative high school teachers with whom we spoke noted that although many new teachers have good intentions, they tend to view students as similar in that they can "fix" any one of them with the right approach. "However, different students take different approaches, and your typical new teacher doesn't have enough choices when working with different types of at-risk or alternative students," said Camille.

"So who is at fault?" we asked.

According to Vicky S. Dill and Delia Stafford-Johnson of the National Center for Alternative Teacher Certification Information at the Haberman Educational Foundation, teacher training programs are at fault.

It's simply wrong to educate teachers generically. Most teacher training programs fail to differentiate for the context in which the teacher will actually ply his or her skills. Can someone who learns to swim at the YMCA in a heated pool greeted with warm fluffy towels at the end of a short session necessarily swim the English Channel? Yet that is the model we currently persist in trying to make them succeed. Traditional teacher certification is like learning to swim at the Y. Nursed along in gradually increasing increments up until several weeks of full-time teaching are attained—usually in the suburbs where it is easy for professors from the local college to supervise—new teachers then are hired to teach at-risk kids. It's like suddenly being asked to swim the English Channel on a stormy day—teaching in the classrooms of the nation's neediest children. (www.altcert.org)

When we shared this passage with Camille, she couldn't help but smile. "I'd have to agree with much of that particular statement, at least as it applies to my alma mater," she said. "Too many of my professors hadn't been in the classroom in forever, and many of their approaches for dealing with the phenomenon they called 'problem' children probably haven't worked since the '60s. And a lot of them weren't up on gender or cultural issues. You have to be culturally aware in so many ways to be successful with at-risk students. You need to be aware of social mores, religious expectations, traditional approaches to life and death, so many things that college courses can't offer."

Olivia concurred with Camille, adding that "experience, though, was my greatest teacher in terms of cultural issues. I mean, I grew up in the Midwest in a predominantly Anglo state and went to a college where few diversity issues besides gender were addressed. But I can't blame my professors for all of that; there were courses I could have taken, but I wasn't interested in them at the time because I hadn't imagined myself teaching in an alternative high school. It's like with so many things in one's life: until you need to know something in order to be a better writer, a better mechanic, you don't see any urgency in learning it. But when I decided to challenge myself with the move to the alternative high school, I gave myself a pretty steep learning curve and went back to school for additional information. I knew what I was looking for—ESL courses, primarily—and had the experience to not only choose wisely but to also better apply what I was learning."

Dill and Stafford-Johnson go on to suggest that "currently there is no endorsement for 'Urban Teaching' or 'At-risk Teaching,' yet there probably should be." Although Tyler thought their approach was a bit extreme (not all alternative schools are in urban areas), he did agree with their general attitude that teachers hired to work with challenging students need to be clear about who they're being hired to teach. "My principal didn't beat around the bush on this at all," he said. "He just said something along the lines of, If you don't have the patience and the commitment to working with these kids, if you can't handle frustration on a regular basis, if you don't have the maturity to worry more about the kids than your own professional needs or desires, you don't belong here. And even though I knew all of those things coming in, even though I had worked at a camp for high-needs kids, it still took so much for me to show up and deal with their disdain and dislike day after day. But I've been here three years, and I'll be here again tomorrow, and that's not going to change. I've adapted because I wanted to and the kids needed me to. It's as simple as that."

What can university programs do to better prepare future teachers for alternative teaching situations? First, those of us working in teacher education need to be clear with our new colleagues about what to expect in at-risk situations or in alternative high schools. This also implies honesty. It can be difficult to tell an idealistic young teacher that she is not ready to handle the realities of an inner-city school in Los Angeles or Chicago. After all, if the student professes to have the qualities necessary to succeed in an alternative high school, are we sure he or she can't handle it? Obviously it depends on the situation. As a third-year teacher who had previously taught in a small rural town in the Midwest, Jean, one of the authors of this book, relocated to a city on the East Coast where she interviewed with a district that was highly multiethnic. After an hour, the principal told Jean that her answers were wonderful, that he loved her enthusiasm, and that if he hired a "white bread" like Jean, the students would destroy her in three days max. Although Jean is still not sure that he was correct in his assessment, he did know his students, and he chose accordingly. In our work with young teachers, teacher educators need to caution those interested in alternative schools about the rigors of the teaching assignment. Also, ideal candidates for alternative school positions have typically gained experience, both in the classroom and in life in general, through travel, additional coursework, and general maturity.

Teacher preparation programs also need to do more to familiarize new teachers with the realities of alternative schools. Most teacher education programs ask students to take part in 40–120 hours' worth of practicums in the forms of observations in a variety of schools. Certainly, if the town or city in which the college is located has an alternative high school, preservice teachers can spend time there. The downside is that typically, the alternative school is fairly small, often with only one or two teachers per subject area; the students may be overwhelmed or resentful if they feel they're being observed regularly by a large number of adults. Asking preservice teachers to watch videotapes (if allowed by the school district) of classroom situations from the alternative school might be a better approach to allowing them to experience and discuss with a veteran teacher some of what happens during a day working with these challenging students.

Furthermore, veteran teachers who have been working with at-risk students should be invited to spend more time in methods courses, talking with education students who may well be qualified for the alternative situation, provided solid mentoring occurs. Anecdotal experiences often help beginning teachers see the situation more clearly, and the opportunity to ask questions about management issues, violence in the classroom, or curricular issues will help clarify the role of teacher at the alternative school.

Finally, many university teacher education programs are reluctant to provide secondary preservice teachers with a semester course titled Classroom Management, mainly because there is no one-size-fits-all approach to disciplinary issues in the classroom. However, a course like this might actually be the ideal place to discuss the differences in managing classrooms in a variety of educational settings. To make this work, however, the teacher-training program would need to use a large number of teachers with a variety of successful experiences in different kinds of classrooms.

Summary

Teaching in alternative educational systems can be immensely rewarding or extremely frustrating. Which one it ends up being depends a great deal on two factors: teacher desire to work with at-risk students and the support of others who have a clear sense of what it takes to be successful in alternative situations. What is absolutely certain is that as long as our society and our educational systems refuse to become more flexible in working with young people, alternative schools are here to stay.

As noted earlier, many of the situations mentors face working with beginning teachers in alternative schools are similar to working with mentees in any first-year situation. However, as our experienced mentors said, discussions of classroom realities, modeling for both beginning teacher and student, and preparing for direct verbal confrontations with students are also necessary components of successful mentoring. In addition, teachers new to the alternative site must be prepared to ask for help, especially if team-teaching situations result in professional discomfort. Finally, university teacher education programs have a part to play in preparing potential teachers of at-risk students. Through practicums and focused coursework, teacher educators may provide their students with a stronger grasp of the attributes necessary for success in alternative schools.

Mentoring to Avoid Burnout

with Susan Kimball and Sarah Brown Wessling

The trials and challenges of beginning teaching—planning units, responding to papers, and negotiating a new school environment—often create conditions for teacher burnout. After years of attending college classes scattered throughout the day, new teachers usually face a schedule beginning in early morning and concluding in late afternoon with the likelihood of several hours of evening homework. This relentless schedule, combined with the insecurity of teaching new material, often causes physical and emotional exhaustion. The special travails of grading periods, parent conferences, and student management sometimes serve as breaking points.

Mentors need to be especially alert for signs of overwork, stress, and/or depression. In *A Place Called School*, John Goodlad (1984) says the typical teacher makes 200 or more decisions per teaching hour. Beginning teachers often experience a mental overload by thinking so quickly so often. At first, all decisions may seem equally important: Which student should I call on first? Should I allow more work time? How do I simultaneously take attendance and get the lesson started? In addition, beginning teachers continually face "firsts": first fire drill, first picture-taking day, first field trip, first parent/teacher conferences, first grading period, first administrator evaluation. As new teachers create a personal management system and adapt to their ever-changing environment, they can start to relax and feel comfortable within their new "home."

Many veteran teachers talk about the challenge and time constraints of teaching one new course. Imagine, then, the complexities of teaching three—

or in small schools, maybe five or six—new preparations and not having a file cabinet filled with time-tested activities. For beginning teachers, many days carry new, unexpected experiences: parental complaints, homecoming preparations, plagiarized essays, or ill students. Almost daily, new teachers must ask themselves, "What do I do now?" The continual bombardment of new experiences, coupled with teaching new material daily, often places the beginning teacher in an ongoing crisis mode. Mentors need to be attuned to these nuances to help prepare beginning faculty members to become more flexible and to rebound from difficult situations without internalizing them.

An important—but often neglected—mentoring role includes nudging and even perhaps pushing the beginning teacher into moving from a passive stance, responding to situations as they occur, to becoming an active participant who makes events happen. The mentor and beginning teacher often, appropriately, focus on survival strategies the first year, but zooming in solely on the individual's classroom sometimes results in a narrow view of the teaching picture. Mentors can help beginning teachers envision a panoramic picture of teaching and learning.

In this chapter, Susan Kimball and Sarah Brown Wessling describe their mentoring relationship during Sarah's first year of teaching. Sarah arrived with an array of field experiences at various schools, a teacher education background based upon Schön's (1983, 1987, 1991) reflective practitioner model, and having co-presented with college professors at state and national conferences. In these ways, Sarah had already stepped into the professional teaching circle. Unfortunately, at that time, the school system had no formalized mentoring program, so Susan first knew Sarah as a colleague and only later gradually moved into a mentoring role. During that momentous first year, Susan helped to develop, refine, and extend Sarah's sense of professionalism through co-participating in workshops, sharing journal articles, and compiling teaching portfolios. Throughout her mentoring experience, Susan employed strategies to maintain Sarah's enthusiasm and prevent the common tendency toward beginning teacher burnout.

Setting the Tone

In the following entry, Susan describes her first meeting with beginning teacher Sarah, which launches them into a year of working together:

Susan: Mentoring Beginnings

It was a hot, hot Saturday morning in late June, so hot, in fact, that I took an uncomfortable risk—going without makeup to school—to meet and talk with a recently hired, first-year teacher about the creative writing course she and I would be teaching that fall. I had hoped to put together a binder of materials but hadn't gotten around to it, so I was feeling ill prepared and inadequate as well as sweaty and plain when I arrived on the sauna-esque, second floor of the high school to be greeted by a composed department head and Sarah, a tall, casually elegant blonde of twentysomething with warm brown eyes and a confident demeanor.

After introductory chitchat, the department chair left, and Sarah and I headed to an air-conditioned room to talk about the course and its à la Atwell structure with choice of topics, genres, lengths, portfolios, and computer lab time for writing. As we talked, I cooled down in the air-conditioning and warmed up to Sarah. Although I'd been blue about saying good-bye to my recently retired colleague who had planned with me for more than twenty years, I was glad to say hello to Sarah, who immediately impressed me as extraordinary, having a knowledgeable acquaintance with writing theory, practice, gurus, and strategies, as well as a firmly constructed philosophy of education. In fact, I could hardly believe that someone so young, so new to the field of teaching, could speak with such authority about so much. I sensed a soul mate, a younger version of the me I wished I had been at her age. I enjoyed our conversation so much that I forgot my naked face and spent more time than I'd planned, bouncing ideas around with Sarah, leaving our first meeting with an optimism about the new school year, knowing that I could learn much from this amazing young woman.

Susan highlights Sarah's demeanor and modestly declines mentioning her own important role in making the beginning teacher feel welcomed and invited into the profession. Although she bemoans her own appearance, she effectively sets the tone for a convivial mentoring partnership. As shown by Sarah's perspective in the following entry, Susan's enthusiasm and professionalism helped them form a positive working relationship:

Sarah: Mentoring Beginnings

When I began my journey as a teacher, I remember making a list of goals. Grouped with "have an objective for what the students are going to learn, not what I'm going to teach each day" and "make contact with every student every day" was "find a mentor." It was as if finding a mentor would have been more appropriately placed on a shopping list rather than on a goals-for-teaching catalogue. I knew from having two extraordinary cooperating teachers during student teaching that as a beginning teacher, finding a mentor and beginning a support system would be necessary, nearly vital to my survival that first year.

I had first met Susan on a horribly hot June morning with the kind of Iowa humidity that could drown even the dandelions. As I waited for Susan to arrive, a recent visit to the department's Web page continued to work its way through my consciousness. The screen, etched in my memory, had proclaimed that nearly every member of this department had either published or received an award or continued education scholarship. I was nervous, no, absolutely scared, that I wouldn't live up to the expectations of this department or school. Like the sweat, which was quickly blanketing my forehead that I was too self-conscious to wipe away, these apprehensions clung to me as I waited and shifted.

Susan's welcoming smile set me at such ease, I was finally moved to dab at my moist forehead. In a moment, I was drawn to her eyes, wide with anticipation and probably a hint of the same fear of unknown expectations. That morning, amidst the dust in rooms that had been locked for a month and the sweat that melted from our foreheads, she did the first of many generous acts. She opened up her files and gave me a copy of everything she possessed. Not only did we go through every manila folder in every closet, but we also found a corner to sit and talk. I don't remember each word of our conversation, but the ones I do were prophetic. I told her how I thought I had misread Nancie Atwell's true intentions for a writing workshop on my first read of *In the Middle*. After an explanation, she said, "Yes, I think the first step is trying on someone else's shoes and walking around in them for a while. Then you can decide if that style is right for you, or if you need a different size." Little did I know that I would find myself in a veritable sidewalk sale of shoes throughout the year and that this teacher would be my guide. Susan hadn't yet become my mentor that day, but her generosity had set us on two roads that would undoubtedly converge.

With that first meeting that started on a positive note for both participants—a vital factor for all mentoring partnerships—Susan and Sarah began the first weeks of what became a long-term personal and professional relationship.

Recognizing Early Signs of Teacher Fatigue

Like many beginning teachers, Sarah's zeal to do all and be all as a planner, teacher, and reflective practitioner produced overextended hours of preparation and paper response, resulting in teacher fatigue. Whereas other professions offer beginners a small load and gradually move them into more advanced responsibilities, the teaching profession often fully immerses beginners from the first day, resulting in a sink-or-swim situation. Unfortunately, many new teachers sink under such heavy expectations and often pull themselves to shore, only to leave the profession and test the waters of a new career. Statistics indicate a high attrition rate during the first teaching year, escalating to more than 40 percent of teachers leaving the profession after five years (*Education Week* 2000). Mentors need to be alert to signs of teacher fatigue during these first crucial years.

In the following passage, Susan describes how she observed both Sarah's potential and her possible self-destruction. She notes the early signs of a beginner immersing and overwhelming herself, often resulting in losing sleep, confidence, and perception of the total picture. Astutely aware of these problems, Susan tells how she provided strategies to help Sarah become less engulfed and more enlightened about balancing personal and professional lives.

Susan: Recognizing Teacher Fatigue

In August I was pleased to discover that Sarah and I shared first-hour planning first semester. I felt drawn to her creativity, wisdom, and energy. She often arrived by 6:30 A.M. and didn't leave until 6:30 P.M. or later. She had organized all her materials into binders, created new activities carefully wrapped in plastic page protectors, each sheet reminding her to include multiple intelligences, learning styles, thinking skills, and questioning types in her lessons. I had never seen such carefully crafted, integrated planning. Sarah revised, updated, and supplemented with new ideas all the handouts she had received from the other veterans or me. She also researched her own stories, poems, and articles to teach the themes required by the sophomore curriculum. It was an unbelievable gift to have Sarah's presence in our department, and I felt lucky to be able to have the first hour of the day for our private chats and brainstorming sessions. I wanted to learn all that this young woman had to teach me.

Somewhere near the end of the first several months into the school year, I saw Sarah at the computer during our mutual first-hour planning period. Sarah amazed me—her creativity, her work ethic, her warmth, her knowledge of what good teaching should be. At the same time, though, I worried that a young person with so many gifts might put herself second, or third, or fourth, or at the bottom of her to-do list. I worried because I have struggled with all of that myself, and the struggle has been, for the most part, a lonely and ongoing one. I didn't know if I dared to tell her that I worried about her, that I was afraid she'd use herself up trying to do all the right things for her students, but not listen to the voice inside that said, "What about me? Don't I need rest, fun, time off for good behavior?"

That day I decided to take the risk and tell her. We'd had many previous conversations about curriculum and philosophy, but I'd never dared to say anything as blunt, as intrusive as "Sarah, I'm concerned that you're going to use yourself up if you keep working as hard as you are, putting the pressure on yourself to be perfect in every aspect of your teaching. I don't want to see you leave the profession in several years because it's too much, because you have no balance between the work and your life. You've got more background knowledge of teaching than many who have taught for twenty years. You have so much to give, but you must not forget to give to yourself. Give yourself time to grow over the space of a career."

I hoped I had not gone too far in saying this, but I had wished many times that I'd had someone to talk to me, express concern for me during my first, horrible years of teaching. In a way, perhaps I was talking to the younger me in the form of Sarah, reminding myself at the same time that this balance issue was one I needed to continue to address in my own professional life.

Although mentoring conferences need to consist of evaluating appropriate activities, discussing special students, and analyzing assessments, mentors also should be willing to veer beyond the typical school agenda and look at the total development of the emerging teacher. In addition to noting the need to help our students grow socially, physically, intellectually, and emotionally, we should be alert to signs that the beginning teacher is becoming consumed by the job and is not nourishing his or her personal, private needs. Just as Sarah may have been surprised by Susan's comments, many beginning teachers do not have enough experience to see how they may be entangling or endangering themselves.

Often, assertive comments balanced by empathetic concern can help beginning teachers become more objective about their involvement and create a more balanced perspective. Susan encouraged Sarah to "give to herself," a wise suggestion since many beginners do not realize that they are giving only "of" themselves and not "to" themselves. Suggestions about one's personal life may include devoting at least one evening per week to personal enjoyment: seeing movies, reading for pleasure, being with friends.

Mentors may find it easy to provide solutions, but it is even more helpful to invite beginning teachers to discuss their own concerns, turning time into an ally rather than an opponent. Mentors may ask questions such as "How could you give yourself more personal time? How would you like to spend that personal time? How could you use time to benefit you as an individual as well as a teacher?" With time divided appropriately between personal and professional lives, beginning teachers can start the school day refreshed rather than frazzled. Susan not only observed Sarah's early fatigue symptoms, but acted upon her intuitive perceptions by discussing the issue in an assertive but nonconfrontational manner.

From her professional reading and intuitive feelings, Sarah realized the importance of discovering a mentor, an individual who could guide and propel her into becoming an effective classroom teacher. Even though Susan's mentor status was unofficial, most schools today offer some form of mentoring program. For Sarah, seeing that someone cared about her as a person as well as a teacher cemented her desire to have Susan serve as her mentor. Without actually using the term *mentoring*, the two colleagues began their year-long journey of growing professionally and personally.

Professional Conferences: Growing Together

Another mentoring role consists of engaging the beginning teacher in the larger picture of the profession. Many beginning teachers become so immersed in day-to-day classroom situations that they may not recognize the totality of the school experience within the department, the building, the district, or the profession. Local, state, and national conferences can help all teachers—especially beginning teachers—step out of the classroom and obtain a panoramic perspective on teaching and learning.

In the following journal entry, Susan describes the personal revival she receives from conferences and her desire to give Sarah that same renewal:

Susan: Conference Vitality

That fall, one of my goals was to attend the National Council of Teachers of English Conference (NCTE) in Nashville. I knew it would be expensive, that our meager English department budget couldn't stretch to pay my entire way, but I had to ask. It would be only the second national conference of my teaching career of more than twenty-five years. After the first national conference, I returned home loaded with ideas, free books, addresses, and a sense that I belonged to a national community of lifelong learners. Through attending local university and state conferences, I had, over the years, heard Nancie Atwell, Toby Fulweiler, Peter Elbow, Chris Crutcher, Ralph Fletcher, Linda Flower, Gary Paulsen, Margaret Atwood, and others. My thinking, teaching, being had changed as a result.

I wanted Sarah to discover the richness and renewal of such professional experiences. Also, I must confess, I was looking for a colleague who wanted to share the conference adventure. Sarah had already participated in and presented at a national spring NCTE conference while a college student, so she knew of the excitement and energy sparked by conferences. However, as a new teacher, she was reluctant to ask for a professional day. She didn't want to appear too demanding, too greedy, especially since other department members, mostly veteran teachers, refrained from asking for conference leave.

Sarah, though, was interested, excited, but concerned about her finances, as were most first-year teachers, trying to balance loan payments with living expenses. I realized I was asking a lot in requesting two days off and $250 of the $350 English budget—meant to stretch over the needs of twelve faculty members—to cover a portion of the more than $600 trip to Nashville, but I finally received permission.

Although most English teachers understand the benefits, attending a conference or a convention costs time, energy, and money. My advice to Sarah was to ask, ask, ask. Find teachers from other schools to room with, travel with, learn from. A true professional needs the stimulation of other professionals. There was always next year and another chance to fight the fight for professional growth.

Conferences, such as the one that Susan describes, can be rich resources to help all teachers—beginning and veteran—be renewed and refreshed, as well as to mature as professional educators. Whether teachers return with new ideas or with reassurance about current teaching practices, the conference time can serve as a retreat to become reenergized and to grow professionally in teaching and learning.

Unfortunately, many beginning teachers are reluctant to ask for professional leave. Administrators, often thinking of costs, may not encourage beginning teachers to attend conferences, and many times they bestow the honor on experienced, hardworking teachers or struggling teachers needing new ways of perceiving teaching and learning. These individuals deserve time to grow professionally, but beginning teachers also need collegial and professional development experiences. Even though conferences and other professional opportunities may be expensive, the costs are even higher when beginning teachers leave the profession. Professional conferences may be one way to foster professional growth and slow the rate of attrition.

Workshops for Professional Growth

Just as conferences can aid professional development, short workshops can help teachers consider new strategies and encourage deeper thinking about teaching practice. If mentors and beginning teachers attend together, they can discuss the proposed ideas and analyze how to apply them to their classrooms. Although many beginning teachers may claim that they don't have time for workshops, they need to evaluate how they are using their available time.

At the end of the first semester, Sarah discovered the overwhelming challenge of simultaneously attempting to respond to papers, tabulate grades, and start new courses. After a week of little to no sleep each night, she wondered, "How do teachers do this? What do I need to do differently?"

Fortunately, both assistance and revitalization arrived in the form of a local school workshop based upon Stephen Covey's book *The Seven Habits of Highly Effective People* (1989). Susan and Sarah attended together, and the two discovered that Covey addresses burnout problems in his third principle: "Put first things first" (p. 145). They noted Covey's advice to make a paradigm shift away from short-term crisis management and toward long-term goal setting by establishing and balancing priorities. Many beginning teachers may see themselves fitting into Covey's Quadrant I of "stress, burnout, crisis management, and always putting out fires" (p. 152). Instead Covey encourages a time management plan based on "vision, perspective, balance, discipline, control, and few crises" (p. 154). In the passage below, Susan describes how making time for the workshop enabled her and Sarah to discover new ways to think about time:

Susan: Covey Training

Later that fall we learned that a districtwide training would be available for teachers during the second semester to study Covey's *Seven Habits* in six half-day meetings. Sarah and I immediately signed up. I was looking forward to some time for self-reflection and discussion. Those days became especially wonderful because Sarah and I got to be partners during class and talk our way through lunch breaks. In our chats about putting "first things first," thinking "win-win," and making deposits and withdrawals to "emotional bank accounts," topics we hadn't previously discussed came rolling out. Our relationship deepened, and we shared mutual hurts, problems, perceptions. We were now friends as well as colleagues.

One of the issues that reverberated most deeply for me, and I think for Sarah, was Covey's "putting first things first." I rediscovered that, for most of my teaching career, I had allowed my work to come before my life. Somehow I hadn't yet accepted Covey's message, "The key is not to prioritize your schedule but to schedule your priorities." As a result, I had managed time in unproductive ways, putting deadline-driven projects, meetings, requests in my "urgent" quadrant and feeling guilty about spending time building relationships, planning, and participating in personal renewal. I shouldn't read that latest best-seller because the paper pile never petered out, and I couldn't plug in exercise as a never-to-be-canceled priority because meetings popped up each week with little advance notice.

But here we were in a district-sanctioned, leadership seminar being told that it was OK, necessary, even more effective to put self into the time matrix, that we'd be "sharpening the saw" by doing so—a lesson that I still needed to build in and that Sarah could learn early in her career before the "shoulds" snapped at her and the guilties got her. What a gift to hear this material together, and to discuss ways to renew ourselves physically, mentally, spiritually, socially, and emotionally. Covey's principles had not been around during my teacher training, had not occurred to me until the last ten years, but how vital they are to a young teacher's repertoire.

This workshop provided a chance for the two teachers to talk about time—an important but seemingly decreasing commodity for all teachers. As Sarah describes in the following journal entry, the togetherness allowed the two to authenticate their mentoring relationship.

Sarah: Covey Training

Since Susan and I were the only high school representatives at the Covey workshop, I had the opportunity to meet excellent teachers from different buildings in the district. I felt part of more than just my own classroom, more than a member of the English department, more than staff at the high school; by interacting with all of these teachers I was part of a district, of a team of many teachers who were all interested in working together to help students learn more effectively.

One element of this program was to formulate a partnership with someone in your building with whom you could periodically discuss how the Covey training was working in the classroom and in life. It was this incidental partnership that finally allowed Susan and me to call ourselves "mentor and mentee" and meet on a regular basis with a sketchy discussion agenda. During these casual yet intensely reflective sessions, we worked to implement our personal goals. By plotting on Covey's Time Management Matrix how I spent my time, I began to learn about the balance Susan had insistently encouraged me to reflect upon. I started to come to terms with the guilt I felt for spending time on nonschool activities.

For example, instead of putting reading for pleasure during the week in the "not urgent/not important" category as an "escape" activity, I was able to see that this was essential to my rejuvenation as a person and as a teacher. The more closely I looked at the activities I considered to be trivial, the more I understood that exercising, journal writing, seeing a movie, or attending a lecture at the local university were empowering for me and that they ultimately helped build stronger relationships with my students and colleagues because I was developing as a distinct individual. These deviations were energizing, and all had characteristics I could draw on in various teaching situations. I realized that I am not only teaching a subject matter, I am teaching who I am and these apparently "frivolous diversions" were extensions of my role in the classroom. I bargained with guilt for entitlement and inspiration.

Unknowingly, Sarah and Susan discovered that the Covey training helped Sarah place the stresses of a beginning-year teacher in perspective. The workshop added validity to Susan's former advice and gave credence to the developing mentor relationship.

Sharing Professional Journals

In addition to conferences and workshops, Susan and Sarah used professional journals as a resource in their mentoring conferences. As an outgrowth of the Covey workshop, Susan talks about how she shared an article on balancing priorities:

Susan: Sharing Articles

It was wonderful to have someone new in the department who liked to talk about professional reading and who had done so much of it so early in her career. I particularly remember the article "Maintaining a Life" by Margaret Metzger I gave Sarah. I thought it was perfect to remind beginning teachers and myself that "You cannot be a good teacher unless you are reading books, going to the movies, spending time alone, and maintaining a life. In order to give to others, you must take care of yourself. Teachers who generously support other people's growth also need to nurture themselves."

I wanted to share this valuable lesson with Sarah, a lesson in balance I had to continually practice to keep my own equilibrium. If I found busyness hard to juggle after more than twenty-five years of teaching English, I couldn't imagine how a young person would cope without someone there to spot her. I wanted to share something I hadn't heard until I started work on my M.A. in my forties: we teach who we are. To me that was revolutionary because it meant that everything I did to make myself a better person—physically, mentally, emotionally, spiritually—made me a better teacher. I wanted to give Sarah the permission I was afraid she wouldn't give herself, that so often I forgot to give myself: consider each teaching day as a working draft, not published perfection. Trust that who you are as a person shines through in all you do. Cherish that person, reward her, be gentle with her.

The sharing of this article and other publications filled a void in Sarah's life. Though eager to start her master's degree, she had decided to postpone graduate courses so she could devote her first year solely to teaching. However, with no interdisciplinary team and few departmental meetings, she often found herself isolated, feeling as if she were part of what Lortie (1975) calls "egg crate classrooms" with sometimes little "real" communication among teachers. Susan encouraged Sarah to discover new collegial friendships by eating lunch in different places so that she could be exposed to different voices. She also showed Sarah how to use the interlibrary loan system so that she could peruse and read books cited in journals. Whether it was sharing information or nudging her toward collegiality, Susan constantly encouraged Sarah to consider new viewpoints and to grow professionally.

Professional Teacher Portfolios

Like other teachers with busy schedules, Sarah discovered the challenge of maintaining both a personal and a professional life. In February, she shared with her English-department colleagues the exciting news of her engagement and upcoming June wedding. This momentous event brought innumerable joys, but it also carried an additional time commitment. Added to the trials and potential burnout of a beginning-teaching year, Sarah decided upon the caterer, florist, and photographer. Lists of wedding "to-dos" lay next to stacks of students' papers awaiting responses. Always the efficient planner, Sarah sandwiched addressing wedding invitations in the midst of lesson planning.

Her upcoming married life included more changes: moving across the state and reinitiating the job search. Securing a different teaching position required updating her resumé and letter of application, typing application forms, and revising her teacher portfolio. Creating a professional teaching portfolio for teaching interviews or for professional growth has become commonplace (Campbell, Cignetti, Melenyzer, Nettles, and Wyman 1997; Glatthorn 1996; McLaughlin and Vogt 1996; Rogers and Danielson 1996; Wilcox and Tomei 1999).

When Sarah reexamined the teacher portfolio created during her student teaching experience, she realized that rather than adding to it, she preferred to reorganize it. As she reread her teaching philosophy, she recognized how much she had matured and grown professionally as a teacher. Given her new insights, she decided to revise her organizational format, as well as add new information. With her typical gusto, Sarah plunged into collecting student paper examples, selecting appropriate journal entries, and composing reflections on varied experiences.

To Susan, Sarah's portfolio proved to be one of the year's highlights. As a continual learner, Susan immediately recognized that she could simultaneously ask questions to help Sarah think through the process and help herself learn a new way to show teacher growth. She asked Sarah a series of questions: "Why did you organize this by these themes? Why did you put the sections in this order? Why did you include these examples of student work? How do these quotes on the title pages represent the work in the section?" In answering Susan's questions, Sarah unearthed many of her teaching philosophies, allowing her to practice potential interview responses and to gain confidence in her portfolio decisions.

With the thought of National Board Certification as a future possibility, Susan listened hungrily as Sarah described the portfolio process. Below she recounts this dual learning process:

Susan: *Professional Portfolios*

During a break in parent/teacher conferences in early April, Sarah shared her portfolio with my student teacher and me and asked if we had any advice for revising it. I was fascinated because I was considering working for my National Board Certification, which required compiling a portfolio of teaching and because I wanted my student teacher to see what an excellent example looked like. Sarah's portfolio was impressive, with quotes to highlight various sections, a pleasing variety of materials to show Sarah's expertise, and a professional quality to all the documents. The only suggestion I could make was that perhaps she could get a parent to supply evidence of her successful teaching. I was happy I could help with a small idea to make an exceptional teacher's work evident for all who saw her portfolio.

The concept of a teacher collecting evidence of her teaching with copies of assignments, student examples, student reflections, colleagues' reactions, and a presentation of her philosophy of teaching seemed so obviously a necessary part of the package of professionalism. Here was a way to document, to save. Why aren't all of us encouraged and supported to develop teaching portfolios? Seeing Sarah's portfolio added one more reason to my growing list of pros for attempting National Board Certification. I'd have a mandate to produce my own portfolio at a time in my life when retirement had become a not-so-distant glimmer. I could think of no more fitting final chapter to the draft of my career than a portfolio of my teaching life.

Although Sarah's portfolio work fostered a rewarding way of viewing her own growth as an educator, it simultaneously created one more daunting task for an already overworked beginning teacher. The end of the school year held a host of burnout potential: another grading period, packing a classroom and a home, job searching, and coping with leaving and restarting.

With the aid of her teaching portfolio, her professional manner, and a year's worth of experiences and reflections with Susan, Sarah garnered a teaching position with her first interview. In beginning her second year of teaching, she realized she was once again a first-year teacher in navigating yet another school system. Her new school did provide an official mentor who helped smooth some of the rough contours of beginning teaching. In the entry below, Sarah describes how she continued to feel Susan's mentoring presence and recall her wisdom on avoiding teacher burnout even as she moved to a new location:

Sarah: Susan's Continuing Influence

During my first year in a new school district, I took Susan's advice that if you want to go to conferences and need to go, then find a way to go. That year I had an opportunity to be a presenter at the National Council of Teachers of English conference, but my principal informed me that my presentation days were "sub block-out" days, meaning that all available subs were being used and no professional or personal leave days would be granted. I remembered Susan's advice that "resourcefulness is a virtue in this profession." I researched. I learned that at times teachers in the building would give up their planning period to substitute for monetary reimbursement. I found a schedule of all the teachers and created a spreadsheet showing teachers who would be available each of the days I wanted to be gone. After a few days, I had located all my volunteers. Being concerned about funding, I looked into the staff development program and discovered a conference attendee fund. I wrote a proposal and received the registration payment. Later, I shared my story with Susan over a phone conversation and could tell she was proud of me. She had set an example of perseverance the year before for all teachers who know this type of professional development is vital to their continued growth.

Overall Reflections

Just as Sarah talks about how Susan influenced her, Susan notes the reciprocity of learning from an enthusiastic beginning teacher. In the following selection, she reflects on how this mentoring experience has affected her teaching life:

Susan: Looking Back, Looking Ahead

In *How to Get What You Want and Want What You Have,* John Gray speaks of ten time periods of life. According to his stages, I'm at the giving-back-to-the-world phase, which comes from ages forty-nine to fifty-six. Gray says, "It is the time to continue growing to experience universal love and share it freely. This is the time to help make a difference in the world." As I near the last decade of my career, I want to continue to cut out the unhealthy, co-dependent behaviors of my earlier years and replace them with a new paradigm where competition and martyrdom give way to camaraderie and cooperation. I want to leave a legacy to those who will replace me—my student teachers and the young teachers like Sarah who have remarkable personal gifts the field of teaching needs. When I listen to their concerns and give them pep talks, I'm also talking to myself, helping myself to figure out possibilities, breaking down the loneliness of the teaching life.

I don't have all the answers—nowhere near—and the questions keep metamorphosing and proliferating. But part of my mission statement (à la Covey) is to become what Covey calls a "transition figure," a person "who breaks unhealthy, harmful, abusive or unfortunate learned behaviors and replaces them with proactive, helpful, effective behaviors . . . modeling positive behavior and passing on effective habits that strengthen and build others in positive ways."

That sounds mystical, pretentious, maybe even phony, but sharing with and learning from young people like Sarah helps me stay young-minded, keeps me nurtured as I nurture, and occasionally lets me be recognized as wise (the ego, after all, is hard to suppress). In his most recent book *The Courage to Teach,* Parker Palmer explains that his book is "for teachers who have good days and bad and whose bad days bring the suffering that comes only from something one loves. It is for teachers who refuse to harden their hearts because they love learners, learning, and the teaching life." Working with Sarah during her first year as a teacher of English kept my heart flexible, gave me someone with whom to share good days and bad days and helped me rekindle my love for the teaching life.

Similarly, Sarah felt invigorated by Susan. Even though Sarah's "teacher fatigue" many times almost turned into burnout, Susan's willingness to be a listener, questioner, and promoter of balance helped Sarah maintain her focus on student learning. Susan honored Sarah for the teacher she was and the teacher she was becoming by granting her the most precious of all teacher gifts: time. In the following and final entry, Sarah reflects on the highlights and frustrations of her first teaching year, looking ahead to the many teaching challenges of the future:

Sarah: Looking Back, Looking Ahead

In the last several years, through interviews and various teaching situations, many people have asked me why I decided to become a teacher. I tell them that it wasn't a decision, rather it was a realization of something that I must have always known. As a young person there were times when I embraced the idea of becoming a teacher, always wanting to emulate the teaching of those who were currently inspiring me. Of course there were times when I tried to deny this was my calling in life. I became sidetracked when I went through the stage when I wanted to do anything to be different from my mother, who was also a teacher. I toyed with aspirations of finding a job that would provide monetary rewards, which I shallowly perceived to be the merits of success. Eventually, I was forced to turn a discerning eye on myself and evaluate who I really was. It didn't take long to uncover what I had always known; I was meant to be a teacher. If I couldn't share my passions of learning and language; if I couldn't proliferate the lessons I'd learned from people like John Keats and Nikki Giovanni, Nancie Atwell or Donald Graves; if I couldn't do work that could carry on in the lives of others, there would be no reason to be.

I left my first year of teaching the way you step off a roller coaster, exhilarated and impassioned from the ride that was smooth and tumultuous so often, so quickly, and so simultaneously that you're not sure when you're climbing or falling. The world I knew was different than how I had known it standing in line waiting my turn. I felt windblown from adventure and excitement, hopeful for the same euphoria and confusion on my next turn. The end of the ride was bittersweet, knowing that I would be on a different coaster with new passengers the next year. I believe the most powerful teachers are the ones who continue to teach even when they are absent. These are the people whose presence resides in our consciousness and our decisions, our reflections and our practices. Susan has continued to be an influence on me as I've worked through the adversities of acclimating to a new school district and the constant questioning that comes from the reflection we so adamantly pursued. I've worked to construct a network of professional learners in my current school in hopes of mirroring the relationship Susan and I cultivated last year. E-mail and phone conversations have kept the two of us easily connected and have continued to host our brutally honest and unabated conversations. I've also been able to look beyond myself as the mentee this year and try to emulate for a few, equally new teachers the type of patience and understanding Susan so often forfeited to me.

I yearn to be a visionary, yet realize I'm still in the neophyte stages of this kind of maturation. Even now I work toward creating my own vision for learning and teaching. I look to find the kinds of truths young teachers need to hold on to. As I've worked toward more self-reflection this year without Susan across the hall, I've had to work to take a more abstract perception of exceptional teaching and turn it into something more concrete, make it something I can depend on when I'm more isolated in this new system. Some days I've had to mentor myself using the techniques that became nearly second nature in only a year with Susan. I cling to the lessons of careful introspection I learned and have become more independently discerning of my own teaching. I suppose this means that I'm growing and that I'm beginning to weave together all the strings of influence I left at my first teaching job. Some days I step into Susan's shoes, some days I wear my own, and on the really crazy ones, my pair comprises one of each.

My friend Donna sent me a message that I enlarged, printed onto a bright orange piece of paper, and carefully placed in a plastic page protector. She told me I was meant to be a teacher and that I shouldn't forget it. I look at the paper that stands out right before the "inspirational" folder in my desk and often recall the familiar question that asks if you can tell the dancer from the dance. If you are called upon to teach, you know that there is no such thing as a job to go to or work to do. There is simply the life of a learner always in motion, always thinking and creating, always teaching. I was meant to be a teacher, I was meant to know Susan, and I was meant to value and learn from her wisdom.

Summary

Eager, enthusiastic teachers like Sarah need mentors like Susan to help anchor them in the goal of student learning and assist them in establishing a balance between a private and a public life. By alerting beginning teachers to the potential pitfalls of teacher burnout, we can, it is hoped, retain them within the teaching profession. Just as a small spark will be extinguished if it is not continually fueled, so, too, the energy and enthusiasm of beginning teachers may slowly die if mentors and an array of professional opportunities are not present to keep the fire lighted. Similarly, large fires can consume areas, and beginning teachers can become so inflamed with a work passion that their professional life may overtake their private life. To prevent teacher fatigue, mentors can be gentle fire feeders, encouraging and nudging the flame while making sure it doesn't burn out of control. By adopting a questioning and listening stance, mentors can help coach beginning teachers in effective ways to rekindle their passion for teaching and learning.

Self-Mentoring: Coaching Oneself Toward Growth

Nobody has really taken me by the hand. In some ways, it would be nice to have somebody to answer questions and be a resource. But I'm kind of a loner. I like being able to do things in my own way.

Daren, beginning teacher

hether the situation consists of working with a beginning teacher who has an independent spirit or helping the new teacher enrich and extend professional growth, mentors can assist others in becoming what Odell (1990) terms "automentors." From a beginning teacher's standpoint, self-mentoring may result from a lack of consistent support or an independent spirit. Whatever the situation, beginning teachers can—with or without the aid of a mentor—strive to reach a higher level of professional growth.

In this chapter, we look first at how Daren moves through stages of working with multiple mentors, a self-designated mentor, and no mentor, until he becomes a self-mentor (Niday 1996). Then we see how Karen helps Martina move into self-mentoring. In these examples, the two beginning teachers learn to use strategies such as reflection techniques, motivational self-talk, questioning, listening, critical thinking, and risk taking.

Daren: Coaching Oneself

Multiple Mentors

Having attended several different elementary and secondary schools, Daren thought he would have an easy adjustment to teaching sophomore English at Oceanview High School. However, he was surprised when Ann, the department chair, told him that no one in the department had volunteered to mentor him, so "we'll just all mentor you."

During the first weeks of school, various English department members offered Daren help or shared materials and information. Because he appeared to be organized, knowledgeable, and confident, the mentors began approaching Daren's door less often.

After the first month, Daren's department members often asked as they passed him in the hallways, "How are things going?" and Daren noncommittally responded, "Fine." None of the department members offered him either lengthy discussions or probing questions.

As the department chair, Ann stopped by Daren's classroom several times after school, suggesting both practical ideas and initiating theoretical discussions. She viewed herself as a potential rescuer: "If you run into problems, I'll try to help you"; and as a possible resource: "You can just drain me of ideas and use what you want." However, when Daren wanted to include more multicultural literature and asked her about it, he received little or no response and eventually stopped asking questions. Daren felt somewhat disappointed. He had expected his multiple mentors to be an advantage or to be overwhelming, but he hadn't expected to be reduced to no mentors. On the other hand, he decided that at least he could avoid challenges and interrogations and become an independent spirit.

Having multiple mentors can be advantageous for first- or second-year teachers; several mentors can provide more listeners and perspectives. RoAne (1993) encourages having "Mentors of the Moment," which she defines as "mini-mentors for specific endeavors and time slots" (p. 138). Daren's many mentors assisted for short periods of time, providing either an overview of courses or small bits of information.

However, multiple mentors often assume others are providing help. Daren's mentors may have had a variety of reasons for their lack of active support, thinking "someone else will do it," being too busy, or viewing Daren as competent and confident in his teaching. In this case, Daren felt simultaneously disappointed and relieved at the lack of mentoring.

Self-Designated Mentor

Ironically, Daren's teaching problems increased just as the department's mentoring decreased, and Daren turned to Deborah, the media specialist, for resource suggestions. When two students objected to reading a short story with a gay character, Deborah, who had recommended the selection, joined Daren and the two students in meeting with the assistant principal. Afterward, Deborah commended Daren for listening to the students, explaining his rationale for choosing the story, and offering alternatives. She was surprised but pleased when he told her he viewed her as a mentor. However, as the year progressed, Deborah's library remodeling project prevented her from offering him more time, and Daren found himself once more with no mentor.

In this situation Daren felt grateful that Deborah supported him, so he informally referred to her as his mentor. Research suggests that if a beginning teacher selects the mentor, then both participants have a better chance of sharing strong mutual respect (Hardcastle 1988; Odell 1990). Odell claims that choosing one's own mentor increases the "effective mentoring bond" (p. 20), and Hardcastle encourages mentoring formed in an unplanned, spontaneous, natural manner.

In designating a mentor, the beginning teacher often finds one or more experienced teachers who share similar personality or teaching traits and can speak freely and easily with the novice. However, unofficial mentors receive no formal recognition, pay incentives, release time, or mentoring professional development, so whenever other professional or personal factors require their time, they often unconsciously abandon what they may not even have viewed as mentoring. If the mentoring situation for some reason collapses— or if the mentor wishes to enhance the beginning teacher's reflective process—self-mentoring may become a viable option.

Self-Mentoring: Using Reflection and Self-Talk

Desiring a multicultural curriculum, Daren requested and received permission to teach the required units in his own way. While the rest of the department taught the traditional Greek mythology, Daren's students explored world mythology. Because others didn't share his curricular values, Daren began relying on self-reflection. However, when students made derogatory comments to others in the hallway, he told himself, "I can't let this go." He took immediate action, talking to the students about the inappropriateness of their language and the need for tolerance of all individuals. Then as a "safety net" to prevent student or parent concerns, he reported the incident to the principal.

Daren's immediate reflection and action constitutes what Schön (1987) calls "reflection-in-action." In this type of reflection, the teacher determines what is happening in the classroom and instantly decides upon and carries out an action. The teacher must assess, decide the cause(s), brainstorm solutions, analyze the pros and cons of these ideas, and select and act, all within moments. Reflection-in-action may occur when the teacher determines that the students do not understand the content and need further illustrations. Other times, as in this example, reflection-in-action is used in management situations requiring immediate response. Schön refers to this as a high level of reflection because it requires synthesizing large amounts of information in a short amount of time. Daren's methods could be considered reflective of Freirean (1970) ideals of using the curriculum rather than letting it use him. He was a prime candidate for self-talk as he struggled to make decisions, be a change agent, and be ready for those who might oppose his views.

In other instances, Daren contemplated taking action, brainstorming different ways to make students more multiculturally aware, thinking of ways to "stir up" students' thinking. He brainstormed different ideas before settling upon one. The next day he discussed with his classes clothing that depicted Native American images such as chiefs and tomahawks. After several students decided that such clothing was inappropriate, he announced that these items would be banned from his classroom. At first a few students resisted and tested him, but he persisted, and the objectionable clothing soon disappeared. Rather than stop here, Daren tackled the issue with the school's equity committee. The committee members willingly discussed the apparel issue but then dismissed it with no action. Satisfied that he had at least increased awareness, Daren dropped the issue.

In this instance, Daren employed what Schön (1987) refers to as "reflection-for-action," reflecting during the planning period. Rather than waiting for multicultural issues to arise, Daren instigated a discussion of them to encourage students and faculty to think more critically. By contemplating various scenarios, Daren, in effect, used Vygotskian "inner speech" (1978). By talking silently through the rewards and perils of such initiatives, he planned how he would encourage student and faculty dialogue about multicultural issues. His alternative to seeking a mentor was to work through reflective thinking by analyzing issues he wished to challenge and problems he wished to avoid.

Most often Daren reflected by replaying class discussions in his head. During a unit on critical reading of newspaper articles and Internet material, Daren told the students, "All opinions aren't equal." The students challenged his premise, citing their beliefs in equality and fairness. When he told them that some opinions are more informed than others, they still didn't agree.

Daren constantly thought about his curriculum and his students, intertwining teaching and reflective thinking. He wrote in his journal, "I'm never really not thinking about teaching. My teaching is not divorced from my living." As an ongoing reflective thinker, Daren liked the concept of continuous process.

In this instance, Daren first used silence, then self-talk, and finally questioning. Having read many books about spirituality and meditation, especially from East Indian and Native American perspectives, Daren often used silence, contemplation, journal writing, and yoga to help himself see situations more clearly.

For this situation, he used several moments of silence to calm himself so he could approach the topic neutrally. Then he wrote a journal entry by typing on his computer what he thought had happened. Sometimes Daren imagined conversations with former mentors such as Mr. Duggen, his college psychology teacher. Instead of asking himself, "What advice would he give me?," he asked, "What questions would he offer me?" In the midst of his writing, he imagined Mr. Duggen's face and framed a question, asking himself, "How can I go back and reiterate it and make it more experiential?"

As a result of self-talk, Daren provided a real-life example in class of getting a medical opinion from a doctor since people trust a doctor's opinion more than others. He said again that all opinions are not equal, and this time students nodded.

By reflecting on a prior event, Daren used "reflection-upon-action" (Schön 1987). He analyzed the day's discussion, mulling over how he knew students hadn't understood the concept. Perhaps Daren often looked back on events (reflection-upon-action) that led to future plans (reflection-for-action). After realizing what hadn't worked and why, Daren used a combination of critical thinking and questioning to plan how to counteract the situation.

By placing himself in his former mentor's shoes, he could Socratically question himself and then switch to his own persona and consider an appropriate response. In this way, he emotionally distanced himself from the situation. In a sense, then, Daren used the Vygotskian (1978) concept of "inner dialogue" or "inner speech" to internalize a previous mentor's voice and points of view.

Mentors use strategies such as posing questions, generating ideas or alternative courses of direction, responding positively, and offering emotional support. In the absence of a real mentor, Daren used self-mentoring for multiple purposes: as an ongoing process to make questions and sense of one's practice in isolation, as self-talk to generate ideas, and as a form of self-advocacy to feel emotionally assured with decision making. The self-talk helped him reflect on intellectual, curricular issues, and the self-advocacy assisted him with emotional issues. To gain these objectives, Daren turned inward— questioning, reflecting, and contemplating how to handle particular situations. He employed an array of strategies: designating another colleague as a mentor; using reflection to assess, brainstorm, analyze, and act; adapting meditative techniques such as silence, writing in a journal, or yoga; and drawing upon the voice of a past mentor to determine effective questions. Using these meditative and questioning techniques, Daren became a self-mentor, intertwining his professional and personal lives.

Teachers Explore Reflection and Self-Mentoring

In nearly all mentoring situations, the mentor needs to lead the beginning teacher from dependent to independent to interdependent stages (Beebe and Margerison, 1995). Whereas Daren worked at becoming an effective self-mentor, the following sets of conversations show how Karen used various mentoring strategies to guide Martina, a beginning teacher, from being dependent to feeling confident enough to be independent and to work with others interdependently. Karen and Martina negotiate and talk through the possibility of reflection as an avenue to self-mentoring.

Karen: I'm really proud of your professional growth this year.

Martina: Well, I definitely feel more confident now than I did during my first days of teaching. I feel like I've grown this year, too, and I owe it mostly to you. You've been a great mentor.

Karen: Actually, I think I've learned as much from you as you have from me. I've been thinking, though, about the next steps we should take in your professional growth.

Martina: OK. What do you have in mind?

Karen: Well, I'm thinking about retiring after next year. I thought it would be a good idea to teach you how to mentor yourself.

Martina: Mentor myself? (laughs) Well, there's no way I can be as good a mentor as you.

Karen: I'll continue mentoring you next year, and after I retire I'll still be available by phone and e-mail. However, I think you should learn how to develop your own professional thinking. Let's look at it as a way of becoming self-reliant.

Martina: OK, let's try it. Where do we begin?

Karen's upcoming retirement spurs her to consider teaching Martina how to self-mentor; however, this stage is important for every teacher. If beginning teachers turn to their mentors with most of their problems, then they are not learning how to be fully in control of their own teaching. Mentors, such as Karen, need to provide good reasons and adaptable steps for the beginning teacher to develop self-reliance and resiliency.

Questioning

In the previous dialogue, Karen shares positive comments with Martina, leading her to feel successful and confident. In the following dialogue, she guides her into analyzing her mentoring strategies, both for Martina's successful and less successful teaching moments. This simple template can lead the dependent novice into a positive pattern of self-talk and reflection.

Karen: Let's start by figuring out how I have mentored you, and then we can see what traits you need to develop.

Martina: Hmmm. Well, you're a great questioner, a good listener. You also make me think critically.

Karen: That's a good starting point. Let's take it trait by trait and see how we can shift the responsibility from my shoulders to yours. Let's start with questioning. Tell me what kinds of questions I ask that are helpful to you.

Martina: (pauses) This is hard. I haven't thought about things from your perspective before.

Karen: (laughs) Well, that's exactly what I want you to do. I want you to start thinking like a mentor.

Martina: OK, you usually start by asking me what good things have happened this week. That always throws me off because I'm ready to talk about what went wrong, and after I start talking, I realize that a lot did go right.

Karen: (laughs) I'm glad it helps you to think more positively. Then what do I ask?

Martina: Then you ask me what caused those positives to happen. That helps me see how I helped create the situation. Then finally you get around to asking me what could have gone better. After I have explained the situation, you ask me about the underlying causes. After my analysis, you ask what I could do in the future to prevent the situation. I hate that question because I want to focus on the problem instead of the future, but it really does help me to prevent reoccurrences.

Karen: Yes, you begin thinking in long-range rather than short-range terms.

Martina: Then you ask me what solutions I've tried, what I plan to try next, and the pros and cons of each possibility.

Karen: (laughs) I think you have me figured out.

Martina: Then you ask me about my next step and how I will evaluate it.

Karen: So how can you ask these questions of yourself?

Martina: I guess I could write them all down and ask myself each question.

Karen: That's a good idea.

By evaluating effective mentoring traits, Karen is helping Martina step into the mentoring role. The self-mentoring questions in Figure 9.1 provide "jump starts" to assist novice teachers in beginning the self-analysis process.

Listening

Let's watch as Karen and Martina move from questioning to the next level of self-mentoring, listening:

Karen: It sounds like you will be able to handle the questioning role. How about active listening?

Martina: You've got me. How can I question, and talk, and listen?

Karen: How does my role as listener help you?

Figure 9.1 **Self-Mentoring Questions**

1. What good things have happened this week?

2. What caused those positive things to happen?

3. What could have gone better?

4. What are the underlying causes to these problems?

5. What can I do in the future to prevent this situation?

6. What solutions have I tried?

7. What solutions do I plan to try next?

8. What are the pros and cons of each possible solution?

9. What is my next step?

10. How will I evaluate whether or not it is working?

Martina: Sometimes I find that after I talk about the situation, I can come up with my own solutions. I really don't need advice because I've figured it out for myself.

Karen: Precisely—so you're really being a listener already.

Martina: Yes, I guess so, but I think I need a system to make myself be a questioner and a listener. I like to write in my journal, so I guess I could write both the questions and my responses.

Karen: That would be a good way to "listen" to yourself because you can reread what you've written.

Once again Karen guides Martina to use questions and self-talk in analyzing the listener role. Martina's use of writing in her journal may work well for her, but other beginning teachers may wish to experiment with a variety of strategies such as talking into a tape recorder, talking aloud in the shower, or conceptualizing the process during a twenty-minute home-to-school commute. Often the self-questioning can conclude with an action plan; in this case, Martina is willing to attempt writing her self-questions and responses in her journal. Any of these listening methods will help beginning teachers use self-talk to guide themselves toward positive action.

Critical and Creative Thinking

Some beginners may not be ready for self-mentoring until their second, third, or fourth year. The process typically requires teachers to recognize that they can think through appropriate responses. This inward dialogue requires critical and creative thinking.

Martina: OK, I've been working on questioning and listening, so what's the next step to self-mentoring?

Karen: Now we're going to work on critical and creative thinking.

Martina: Sounds difficult.

Karen: Actually, it's rather fun. Let's start with higher-order thinking skills. You know that according to Bloom's taxonomy, the lowest thinking skills are knowledge and comprehension and the next highest skills are application, synthesis, analysis, interpretation, and evaluation.

Martina: Right, I learned all of that in college.

Karen: Well, one of the most important things we can do as teachers is make the content material relevant to students by connecting it with their lives. However, sometimes it's hard to do that. That's when it's helpful to use analogies.

Martina: Could you give me an example?

Karen: Sure. Today I taught my seventh graders about magnetic attraction. I compared it to two people who fall in love at first sight and how they are drawn to each other. Then I taught how magnets repel each other, and I compared it to a couple getting mad at each other and breaking up. Even preteens can understand romance.

Martina: (laughs) You're right!

To help Martina move into critical and creative thinking, Karen gives her a concrete method: using analogies to connect to students' prior experiences. Karen's example of magnetic qualities helps Martina move into new ways of processing how to make content material accessible to students. Analogies use both critical and creative thinking, making them a higher form of thought. Karen also shows Martina how to adopt a critical or judgmental stance for her own teaching, one in which a new teacher can move beyond seeing the good and less successful acts of teaching and analyze new ideas to explore possibilities.

Self-Awareness: Recognizing One's Values

Another important component of self-mentoring is developing the skill of self-awareness. In the following dialogue, Karen prepares Martina for this step toward conscientious teaching:

Martina: I've now started questioning and listening to myself and even forming appropriate analogies for students to connect their past experiences to current learning. What's the next step?

Karen: I think you're ready to tackle self-awareness.

Martina: What does that mean in terms of teaching?

Karen: You're probably already aware of your own and your students' multiple intelligences and learning styles.

Martina: Yes, I try to use a variety of activities and assessments to enable all students to use their talents. I know that I'm a visual and analytical person, but I realize that others may have different ways of learning.

Karen: Right. And the next step is to realize what inhibits our learning.

Martina: Huh?

Karen: We need to be aware of our own values, where they originate, and how they may stop us from processing new information.

Martina: Can you give me an example?

Karen: Sometimes we characterize someone who doesn't complete an assignment as lazy, someone who cheats as being immoral, or someone who is looking off into space as not paying attention.

Martina: And aren't those true?

Karen: Not always. Maybe the student who didn't complete the assignment had to stay at a friend's house to avoid an alcoholic parent. Maybe the person who cheats didn't understand that particular math chapter because the teacher's explanation was inadequate. Maybe the person staring off into space is being attentive but just appears to be oblivious to the class.

Martina: So you're talking about jumping to conclusions before knowing all the facts.

Karen: Yes. There's an old story that J. C. Penney used to invite prospective managers to lunch. If they put salt or pepper on their food before tasting it, he wouldn't hire them because they were making a judgment before they knew all the facts. (Both laugh.) I don't know if that story is true or not, but we all err in making judgments before we know the entire story.

Martina: So I should be aware of my own value system and prejudices. Well, I guess I was the good student and always turned in my assignments on time, so it's hard for me to understand why others don't attempt to do their work. It just makes me mad.

Karen: Have you attempted to discover why students may not be finishing their homework?

Martina: Sometimes. I probably should do it more often. As for the student with the alcoholic parent, that probably wouldn't occur to me since my own parents didn't have addictions. I have a lot to think about.

In this instance, Karen helps Martina realize that self-awareness is key in examining and sometimes reexamining values to see beyond our own histories. Marlys Mayfield (2001) describes self-awareness as resisting the impulse to stereotype, jump to conclusions, or take things for granted. According to Mayfield, self-aware individuals analyze their value systems to discover what they believe to be true and fair. Then they check for evidence and valid reasoning. To become self-aware, teachers need to consider different perspectives before making judgments and need to question their own beliefs and values.

Exploring and Questioning One's Values

After showing Martina how to recognize her personal value system, Karen is ready to guide her to a higher step of "conscious" teaching by exploring and questioning her values:

Karen: Are you ready to continue toward your goal of becoming a self-mentor?

Martina: I guess. Over the last week I've been thinking about questioning my beliefs.

Karen: OK, we'll continue in that vein. When do you do more reflection: when a teaching day goes well or when you have problems?

Martina: That's easy. When I have a good day, I drive home feeling content and satisfied. On days that I have problems, I spend the drive home thinking about what happened and why.

Karen: Do you think it would be helpful to analyze why things went right on the good days?

Martina: That's a good idea. Success usually leads to more success, so I should figure out why some things work well and then I can keep doing them.

Karen: Now you're thinking! (Both laugh.) Of course, it's natural to think more about those problem days. We often must be uncomfortable before we can really think deeply.

Martina: I remember now that question two on the self-mentoring sheet was "What caused those positive things to happen?" I've been using those questions, but I have to admit that I've been skipping number two. You've given me more to think about.

Karen: We talked earlier about being a good self-questioner. A good question to ask yourself periodically is "How am I being a risk taker?"

Martina: (laughs) I'll add that to my list.

This scenario reveals our tendency to focus on negative experiences. Karen, in this case, suggests how both positive and negative experiences can be a springboard for analyzing events, and she reminds Martina to question causes and effects. Stephen Brookfield (1987) says critical thinking tends to be sparked by "trigger events," which tend to be negative situations. These circumstances cause us to feel a disequilibrium, and we must deconstruct and rethink what we know without demolishing our own self-esteem. According to Tishman, Perkins, and Jay (1995), we must challenge our assumptions, explore alternatives, and take risks in our thinking.

Group Self-Mentoring: Creative Thinking and Risk Taking

After Karen leads Martina past the disequilibrium stage of questioning old values, she's ready to guide her to new ways of thinking:

Karen: You're doing great as a self-mentor. Now let's try taking an old idea, analyzing it, and then brainstorming new possibilities.

Martina: OK. I think our team meetings are becoming boring. We tend to discuss the same student problems and plan the same end-of-the-year interdisciplinary project. I've been thinking about introducing these self-mentoring concepts to my team. Is that too big of a project?

Karen: Well, you can try it out and see what happens.

Martina: I've heard people say that the best way to learn something is to teach it to others, so maybe by showing others how to be self-mentors, I can learn to be a better self-mentor myself.

Karen: Go for it! I'll be eager to hear what happens.

Two months later:

Karen: We've been assessing your own self-mentoring in our recent conferences, but it also sounds like you have some good things going with your team.

Martina: Yes. I've been using your ideas, and each week I've taught them a different method of self-mentoring. It's kind of like a long retreat. We questioned our old way of doing things. Then for the listening step, we tape-recorded one meeting and played back part of it at the next meeting. We listened for individual and group dynamics. We suddenly realized how we were interrupting each other or veering away from the topic.

Karen: (laughs) Wow, that really is progress.

Martina: I agree. Now the team is thinking about critical and creative thinking. We realized that as a team we usually just solve short-term problems such as the kid who doesn't do homework. That's important, but we wanted to look at the whole picture of student learning. Cameron, our team leader, asked us to think "outside the box" for new ways that our team could function. He encouraged us to go beyond our typical novel or history interdisciplinary units and to brainstorm ideas for a unique end-of-the-year collaborative teaching project. I tossed around different creative ideas overnight, and I decided to propose a roller-coaster unit.

Karen: Well, that's really different. How did you get that idea?

Martina: I thought about prior knowledge and motivation, and I decided that seventh graders know about and like roller coasters.

Karen: That's true. How will the unit work?

Martina: We're still in the planning stages, but we're going to put the kids into groups, give them some materials, and then have them create roller coasters. The math teacher will work with them on measurements and angles; the English teacher will ask them to write a story using a roller coaster as the setting or create a poem in the form of a roller coaster; the social studies teacher will supervise their research on the history of famous roller coasters; and as the science teacher, I will teach them about propulsion and velocity.

Karen: That sounds fun. Are you taking any other risks?

Martina: Yes. Some classes may need more time than others, so we're going to rearrange the schedule for our team.

Karen: Great! Anything else?

Martina: Well, that was my teaching idea. Vicki's idea was for our team to talk about ways to accommodate second-language learners and use their talents. We looked at our old beliefs and found that we often thought, "We haven't been trained in that area. That's the ESL teacher's job." We decided that maybe we need to be learners, too, so next year our team is going to ask our ESL coordinator to choose a professional book for us to read. Then we're going to do a team action research project and try some different strategies with second-language students and see what we can learn.

Karen: What problems do you foresee?

Martina: Probably lots. Next fall we may not have the enthusiasm for this project like we do now. We're also going to have to figure out how to balance short-range things like individual student problems with long-range ideas like this self-study. I don't know if we can do both. I guess we'll have to try it and use your list of questions. It's harder for a team to do self-mentoring, but it's definitely more fun.

Karen: Your team members are now doing both self- and peer mentoring. It looks like you're off to a good start.

Like all teachers, Karen is excited when Martina carries the concept of self-mentoring a step further and begins teaching her team. Through her questioning, Karen helps Martina define what has happened with the team and what has and hasn't worked.

To create disequilibrium, teachers sometimes have to reorganize their schema or challenge conformity. For instance, Martina's team realizes that at the end of a school year, teachers often want to squeeze in more content at the same time that students often wish to do less work. Cameron, as the team leader, calls for creative, risk-taking approaches, and the resulting idea of a roller-coaster unit allows teachers to review and introduce new concepts while providing student motivation.

Similarly, many teams get so entangled with individual problems that they often ignore the big picture of overall student learning. Martina's team decides to retain but narrow down their system of assessing individual problems and take time to explore the special challenges that second-language learners face. Her team members adopt an open-minded attitude that supports collaborative learning. Like Martina, the team will need to monitor its progress as they collectively meet successes, frustrations, and challenges. Just as an individual's self-mentoring requires self-discipline, group self-mentoring can be equally challenging, but the results can be even more rewarding.

Summary

Self-mentoring allows teachers to grow professionally through being reflective about their own beliefs and practices. Some teachers, such as Daren, may become self-mentors when they don't have a mentor or when, like Martina, they wish to explore their own reflective thinking.

Daren used reflection as a form of talk for curricular issues and as a means of advocacy for emotional issues. He tried designating another colleague as a mentor; using meditative techniques such as silence, writing in his journal, or yoga; and calling upon the questioning talents of a past mentor. By becoming a self-mentor, he intertwined his professional and personal life.

Karen helped Martina become a self-mentor through developing her questioning and listening. Martina expanded her repertoire of critical thinking skills by using self-awareness, recognizing and exploring her values, and taking risks. Martina even decided to try a greater challenge, expanding the concept to a team level. A team's self-mentoring can function like an ongoing retreat, constantly monitoring and assessing old practices, as well as exploring new channels.

By becoming self-mentors, all teachers can expand their reflective thinking. By viewing their beliefs and practices through new perspectives, questioning former pedagogical practices, and attempting a team action research project, they can creatively consider how to help students learn.

Mentoring the Teacher
Who Struggles

"During third period I walked past your classroom on the way to the office, and I saw students leaning forward in their seats and waving their hands to participate. It looked exciting. What was going on?" Lorraine asked Becca, a beginning teacher.

Becca looked up from her lunch, surprised. "Well, we were brainstorming ideas about how we might show what we learned about the Egyptian pyramids. The students had really good ideas. I'm eager to see them get started on their group projects."

Lorraine grinned. "It sounds like you've got your students enthusiastic about learning. What a great accomplishment!"

Becca hesitated, then acknowledged, "We did have a good discussion that period."

"I guess so. Just seeing all of that excitement made me want to be one of your students."

"Really?" Becca asked.

"You most certainly had their attention and involvement."

As the two continued eating, Becca glowed in the sincere comment from her more experienced colleague. She visualized what Lorraine had described—students leaning forward and hands wildly waving—and repeated to herself Lorraine's positive words. Becca knew that too often, she dwelled on the negative experiences she had been having with her first- and second-hour classes. Lorraine's words of praise gave her a new perspective. Something did go right today. Maybe she was meant to be a teacher after all. She entered her next class period with a new sense of confidence and self-worth.

All beginning teachers encounter challenges within the first years of teaching, but some struggle more than others. Different strategies may be needed to help the at-risk beginning teacher achieve success, especially if the beginner has little confidence or, worse, denies having any problems. Inevitably, a few discover that a teaching career is not compatible with their talents and personalities; these individuals require direct intervention or counseling to help them find other professions. In this chapter, we analyze various reasons why early career teachers struggle, consider strategies to encourage individuals to stay in the profession, and offer methods to assist those lacking in skills. Finally, we propose ways to use tactful, professional conversations to encourage those not meant to be in the profession to find another career.

Lack of Confidence

Sociologists often refer to Cooley's looking-glass theory (Canfield 1990), a long-held sociological belief that we visualize ourselves in the way that we think others see us. Lorraine's comments served as a mirror, showing Becca how her more experienced colleague viewed her. When beginning teachers hear veteran colleagues praise their work, they begin to see themselves as valued educators who can make genuine contributions to the profession. As sociologists tell us, sometimes our self-mirrors lie or provide us with only a partial picture. Lorraine's comment gave Becca a new mirror, a different perspective, a positive vision of who she was and who she could become.

Just as parents employ the concept of "Catch them while they're good" with their children, mentors can use the same philosophy. By looking for positive moments, Lorraine helped Becca rethink her self-image. That evening Becca went home recalling Lorraine's words: "I saw students leaning forward in their seats and waving their hands." She especially treasured Lorraine's statement: "Seeing all of that excitement made me want to be one of your students." With renewed energy and enthusiasm, Becca looked for examples of active participation instead of being overwhelmed by the few signs of apathy. Mentors need to help beginning teachers be patient with themselves to realize their visions of effective teaching.

Inadequate Planning

"So how did your first week go, Jared?"

"Well, I thought I had planned the first two weeks of school, but my earth science class finished everything in four days."

Marvin chuckled. "You know, almost the same thing happened to me in my first year of teaching."

"Really?"

"Yup. I had trouble getting the kids to talk at first, so I just kept moving on to the next topic."

"That's exactly what happened to me," Jared said, amazed. "So what did you do?"

"Well, first I asked myself why it was happening. So let me ask you: why do you think the kids were so silent?"

Jared thought for a few moments and finally shrugged his shoulders. "I don't have the faintest idea. I didn't expect this at all. Why do they do that?"

"Well, I learned that high school kids often feel uncomfortable at the beginning of the semester. They think they know an answer, but they're not sure that it's the teacher's 'right answer,' so they freeze up. Besides, they don't want to be a know-it-all in front of their peers, especially if they don't know the other kids in class."

"I hadn't thought about that. I thought it was just me not asking the right questions. So what did you do?" Jared repeated.

"One time someone told me about think-pair-share, and I found it works pretty well. You first give kids a topic to write about, then you have them share with a partner, and then you ask them to share what they or their partner said. That way the student feels good because it's kind of a joint answer. When they've written and spoken about it with someone else, they've already rehearsed what they want to say, so they feel more comfortable repeating it."

"Oh, yeah, I learned about that at college. I should try that."

"You might also try putting them in groups. Then they can have a group spokesperson. That should loosen them up, too."

"Uh-huh. For some reason, I thought I needed to lecture and prove to them that I know this subject. I guess that's not true."

Marvin laughed. "Don't worry, you'll get the hang of it. What good things have happened?"

"Not much," Jared replied dolefully. "Yesterday I didn't have enough planned, so I told them they could have the last ten minutes to talk. They sure proved they could talk! They kept getting louder and louder and people started yelling across the room at each other. I was just waiting for some other teacher or Mr. Phelps [the principal] to come in and yell at us for being so loud. So today, even though I didn't tell them they could have free time at the end of class, a couple of kids got up to stand by the door about five minutes before the bell. And once they did it, everybody did it. It was OK until one kid punched another kid, and then, thankfully, the bell rang."

"Wow," said Marvin. "Sounds like it got a bit out of hand. What are you going to do tomorrow?"

"I guess I need to tell them that the class isn't over until I say it's over. And I definitely need to plan the class right up to when the bell rings, so they can't get off task."

Marvin smiled. "It sounds like you're learning quite a lot, Jared."

Inadequate planning often creates myriad problems. Many beginning teachers don't have a sense of the time required for a particular activity; it is not uncommon for them to discover that their hour's worth of material takes only twenty minutes to complete. Whereas an experienced teacher possesses a repertoire of examples or can extend a discussion with effective questioning, a beginning teacher often cannot think of additional illustrations or doesn't know how to guide a discussion into new areas. In the initial weeks of a semester or any time a new teacher enters the picture, students may be wary of giving comments until they feel comfortable in the environment. Mentors can encourage beginning teachers to "overplan" so that they use every minute of the class period or, as Jared calls it, "teach until the bell rings."

As an experienced mentor, Marvin employed the question-and-listen technique. Early in the conversation, Marvin could sense Jared's sense of desperation in his negative responses to Marvin's initial question of "So how did things go this week?" and his later positively phrased "What good things have happened?" Like many beginning teachers, Jared immediately dismissed the positives and started relating all of the negatives. Realizing Jared's need for—and lack of—effective instructional strategies, Marvin offered the techniques of think-pair-share and cooperative learning. It is important for mentors to help beginning teachers think through situations and arrive at their own answers, but when mentors see that the novice is struggling, they must throw out a lifeline before returning to their listening-and-questioning stance.

As Jared discovered, ineffective planning can lead to classroom management problems. If students aren't busy, they often resort to other means of entertainment.

Classroom Management

Jeff, a second-year teacher, looked over at his mentor, Lionel, and gave him a quick thumbs-up. Jeff was new to Mountain Edge Middle School after having taught in Happy Valley High School for a year. Happy Valley had been an upper-class, well-financed school with an extremely homogeneous student population. Mountain Edge was socioculturally diverse, and Jeff had quickly found that he needed different methodological approaches with the wider variety of students; he also found that management took on a different look in his new school. At first, Jeff tried to differentiate his management plan himself, but after a frustrating two weeks, he sheepishly went in to talk to Lionel and to admit that he felt like he was in over his head.

Lionel listened intently, then asked if he could come in and observe Jeff's class during his prep hour the following day. Lionel observed Jeff's fourth-hour class, then met with his mentee after school. The two men discussed what Jeff thought he was doing in terms of management and what Lionel had actually observed during the class period. Then they began to work on a modified management plan for Jeff to try during fourth hour the following day.

Although Jeff encountered some rough moments over the next week, he found Lionel's suggestions to be good ones, and within two weeks thought his modified management plan was working effectively for both himself and his students.

As we note in *Mentoring Beginning Teachers,* most teachers do not go into education because they look forward to classroom management issues. University teacher preparation programs can provide support for preservice teachers in researching and critiquing various management plans, but the reality of dealing with classroom disturbances and other related issues are most sensibly dealt with during student teaching. In addition, teachers who move into schools culturally or economically different from the one they student-taught in, like Jeff, may encounter difficulties as they adapt to their new teaching situation.

There are, unfortunately, occasions when beginning teachers are never able to integrate classroom management into what goes on in the classroom. When there has been significant intervention on the part of a mentor and/or administrators and the beginning teacher still cannot manage the classroom in a manner that allows for successful teaching, there must be a serious discussion about that teacher's future in the classroom.

Insufficient Knowledge

Due to a teacher shortage in certain content areas, some beginning teachers have been hired to teach outside their primary discipline. Mentors working with beginning teachers in this situation often have a double responsibility: not only must they take care of the typical responsibilities we discuss throughout this chapter, but they have to support the novice teacher's knowledge development.

Faith: So, William, are you all set for the first day of classes next week?

William: (laughs) No, not by a long shot! The worst thing is, I don't feel like I know my subject. My major was earth science, this job is biology, and they hired me anyway, knowing they would have to request an emergency license. I needed a job: what can I say? I'm beginning to wonder, though, whether I should have taken it. I feel like I can barely swim, and I'm going to be diving off the high board.

Faith: I can see how you feel rather lost. What can I do? Would you like to see some of my biology units?

William: Sure, that would be great. Since I don't know the area very well, I guess I'll follow the textbook pretty closely.

Faith: That's a good idea. Is there anything else you're concerned about?

William: (nods) Uh-huh. I just can't seem to get excited about teaching biology. All this time I've been imagining showing students different rocks and minerals and having them make models of the solar system. Now I have to completely change my way of thinking. I don't like dissecting animals or talking about the human body. And I don't know what to do about the sex ed unit. I'm only a few years older than these students, and some of them probably know a whole lot more than I do.

Faith: (laughs) I'm middle-aged, married, and have three kids. But I'm sure many of them know more than I do, too. Actually, I like teaching that unit because the kids are so . . . motivated. (Both laugh.) Maybe we could move the partition between our rooms and team-teach that unit. You could give the directions for their assignments, and I could lead the discussions. How does that sound?

William: That's great. That makes me feel much better. Thanks, Faith.

Many beginning teachers lack confidence, but when they're teaching outside their area of expertise, it's only natural that they may feel out of their league. This problem is even more severe when, for example, a history major is hired to teach in math or science. In these instances, administrators are wise to assign mentors in the same content area or at least in the same discipline. In addition to helping William negotiate typical school procedures, Faith must help with the content area itself. Her suggestions to share units and team-teach can help a beginning teacher like William find success more easily.

William lacks not only knowledge but also enthusiasm for his new content area. Besides providing content knowledge, Faith may need to share her love for biology. Because enthusiasm is often contagious, William may soon discover another area of science to enjoy. Faith's role as a mentor may be doubly complex, but she has great potential for influencing a beginning teacher and his students.

Lack of Teaching Skills

In this age of teacher shortages, governmental and educational institutions are searching out people to serve as teachers who would not previously have been considered likely candidates. People who sign up with programs such as Teach for America or AmeriCorps or those in alternative licensure programs may encounter difficulties in the classroom because they lack basic teaching skills. Individuals returning from the Peace Corps or other overseas teaching assignments who are not licensed through a state board and are hired in areas where licensing rules can be bent may have had some experience teaching, but often find that the teaching circumstances are quite different. These individuals may possess in-depth content knowledge but probably do not understand students or school life.

Ben: Well, Harold, you've almost completed your first semester. How's it going?

Harold: (chuckles) It sure hasn't been what I expected. Almost everything I pictured has been different.

Ben: What have been your greatest challenges?

Harold: Before I started my own successful business, I was in the army as a communications manager; with that combination, I thought teaching business would be a cinch. I thought all I had to do was tell students everything I've learned through my years in the workforce. Then I found that they would listen to my lectures for only short periods of time. You and the principal have been talking to me about active learning, but I'm used to telling people what to do, not letting them discover it for themselves.

Ben: You have tried some different methods, though, Harold, so that's a start.

Harold: Yeah, but I still can't believe the students' attitudes. I'm used to giving orders and having people comply. These kids don't pay attention half the time and don't turn in their work. I yell at them, but that doesn't seem to do anything either.

Ben: Yelling usually doesn't work.

Harold: It's sure different from what I expected. Even the faculty meetings are problematic for me. I'm not used to this bottom-up approach of teachers making decisions. What do we have administrators for, if not to tell us what to do and when to do it?

Ben: This has been quite a change for you. We've talked about all of these issues and I'm not sure you always appreciate my suggestions.

Harold: Well, you have helped me by telling me why some of my ways don't work. I've been realizing a great deal lately that education is very different from when I was a high school student in the fifties.

Ben: But I have seen some changes in your approaches these last few months.

Harold: I guess so. I'm trying. But in all honesty, I'm not sure I'll be around next year.

Effective teachers need both content and pedagogical knowledge. People who come from the business or work world possess certain types of expertise, but it does not necessarily translate into successful teaching practices. A number of issues must be confronted before individuals interested in midlife career changes attempt to make this transition.

- First, nontraditional teacher hopefuls are often attuned to top-down management styles; these rarely work in school situations.

- Second, most educational experts acknowledge that a constructivist philosophy is necessary for students to be successful in a variety of active learning educational circumstances. Individuals who have not completed a university teacher education program typically do not experience constructivist models and therefore are not always able to provide them in the classroom.

- Third, sharing knowledge is not a substitute for providing students with the objectives for why they are learning certain concepts. Teachers need to provide a purpose for learning and relevance between the content delivered and student needs.

Mentors can assist these beginning teachers in understanding the student population, various learning styles, and effective teaching strategies, but the reality is that these people would fare better if they were expected to complete university teacher preparation courses. Mentors should not be asked to take over the roles that universities have accepted and usually handle quite effectively.

Lack of "Appropriate-Age" People Skills

Cassidy relished being a 4.0 student in English education. Her extensive academic vocabulary enabled her to compose fluent literary critiques. In her methods courses, she easily discussed theoretical implications of practice and created a detailed unit plan on Tolstoy's *Anna Karenina*. As an academic student, Cassidy excelled.

During her practicum experience with an AP senior class, she worked one-on-one with students, helping them with their papers or conducting student book conferences. When students were working in groups, she moved about the room, listening in on and occasionally questioning group members. However, Cassidy's practicum mentor failed to provide an opportunity for Cassidy to plan a lesson or to lead a full-class discussion. Nevertheless, her methods teacher, who also made student teaching placements, thought Cassidy was more than ready to face the challenge of a ninth-grade classroom.

Cassidy's student teaching placement was with Lin, who taught five sections of freshman English. During their first planning session, Cassidy noted, "It's too bad I can't use my *Anna Karenina* unit . . . maybe we could view it as a real challenge to their intellectual growth?" she finished hopefully.

Lin smiled and said she usually began the year with a personal narrative followed by a young adult literature unit.

"Oh, well then, why not let me use *Romeo and Juliet* when we move into the young adult stuff?," Cassidy said. "My methods teacher told me that is the play most often taught at the ninth-grade level."

"I do teach *Romeo and Juliet*, but it typically falls toward the end of the school year," Lin said. "A young adult lit unit can work effectively as a bridge between the students' middle school experiences and what they will be facing in high school. Any ideas for that type of unit?"

When Cassidy shook her head, Lin told her that they could team-teach the personal narrative and that she would give Cassidy a number of books written in first person that would work well as a bridge from the writing unit. Later that evening, Cassidy held five Y.A. lit books in her hands, a disgusted look on her face. "They're all less than 200 pages," she muttered, "and who really cares about the problems of the twentieth-century teenager?"

Over the course of the next four weeks, Cassidy found that ninth graders matched none of her expectations of how high school students should behave. They failed to do their homework and stared when she used phrases such as "temerity of the protagonist" or "between Scylla and Charibdys." She lectured over their heads—literally and figuratively—when she read through five pages of notes on the young adult author Robert Cormier. Because she didn't look at the students while she was lecturing, she didn't notice that one student had crawled out the window until he appeared at her classroom door, escorted by the principal.

Shortly afterward, Lin asked, "Cassidy, do you enjoy coming to school, planning lessons, or working with students?"

"No."

"Do you want to continue in your student teaching?" Lin asked.

"Actually," Cassidy replied, "I've started looking into graduate schools. I don't think the ninth-grade life is for me."

Some preservice teachers may excel in college-level courses, but not be able to experience the same success as an educator. Teacher preparation programs should include several field experiences throughout the college career so that prospective teachers have a better sense of what age or ability level they feel most competent working with. Although practicum experiences, even ones that allow the preservice teacher to plan for a full-class discussion or a number of mini-lessons, cannot ensure that individuals will be successful at the grade level they most desire, they are necessary in providing university students with greater insight into classroom life. Even though Cassidy could talk enthusiastically about working with adolescents, she found that she was not prepared to think below the college level; indeed, she was not willing to shift her thinking to accommodate younger learners. Mentors can teach some acclimation skills, but the prospective teacher must be willing and able to make the adjustments needed to support student learning.

Parental Pressure

Alberto walked into the adjoining fourth-grade classroom of his mentor, wearing a worried expression. "Frances, I just received a message from the office that a parent wants to meet with the principal and me after school."

"What's it about?" Frances inquired.

"It's Mr. Cortizio," Alberto said. "He told the principal that I treat his son, Marc, unfairly."

"What's been going on?"

"Oh, Marc hasn't been doing much work in class, and he's been hitting kids at recess. He talks back to me when I ask him to do things."

"How have you handled it?"

"I've tried talking to him and keeping him in at recess, but his behavior hasn't changed. I've tried looking for the things he does well, but that hasn't helped either. Finally, I called his parents last night."

"Is anything going on at home?"

"Not according to the father; he told me that I'm just not handling his son right. And when I suggested to him that the bullying and general apathy might be a sign of depression or upset at something that's going on in his personal life, his father asked me if I had a license to practice psychology. I apologized for overstepping, but told him that I was calling only because I'm concerned for Marc. He just laughed . . . and not very nicely."

"So how are you going to handle the conference?"

"I don't know, and he's going to be here in half an hour."

"Would you like to practice? I could pretend that I'm Mr. Cortizio, and we could go through some conference scenarios."

"Great. Thanks, Frances."

Working with parents or guardians can be especially challenging for beginning teachers. Making phone calls to parents, participating in open houses and parent/teacher conferences, and responding to e-mails can be taxing when added to other responsibilities. A belligerent parent, like the one Alberto encountered, can overwhelm a new teacher. Inexperience and youth are often apparent through a beginning teacher's nervousness or hesitant manner; a parent may be less likely to question the actions of an older or more experienced teacher. Just as Frances encouraged role playing the conference,

mentors can help beginning teachers think through situations so they can discuss the issues with the parents or guardians in a calm, positive manner.

Overwhelmed

Melinda walked by her new colleague Carina's door. It was 7:30 in the evening and
Melinda had already been home, made supper for her family, and then returned to
school after realizing she had left all of her handouts for the inservice she was facil-
itating at school. She stuck her head in the door. "You're still here, Carina!" She was
about to add a teasing comment about students thinking their teachers live at school
when she noticed tears on the younger teacher's face. "What's wrong?"

"Oh, it's silly, but I promised my American lit students that they would get these
papers back at the end of their class periods today and I didn't make it."

"Well, we all get behind on occasion, Carina, but you shouldn't feel like it's the
end of the world."

Carina smiled wanly. "They're already late, and I made a big deal at the beginning of the year about never holding any of their papers longer than two weeks. So
here I am, with twenty-six papers from my sixth hour left to grade. I just don't know
if I'm up to everything involved in teaching. My professors talked about how much
time was needed to prepare for classes, and they told us to be careful about how
many extracurricular activities we volunteered for. . . ." Carina's voice trailed off.

"Carina, it can be overwhelming at times, and I'll never forget how busy I was
my first year. My principal put me on so many committees and I was too scared to
say anything." Melinda watched as Carina nodded her head in agreement. "I know
that you're also busy with the play right now, but what else is going on?"

"I guess I forgot to tell you that Mr. Simmons [the principal] came to me two
weeks ago and asked me to take over a small-group speech contest; he said Jenny
Graham felt that she just wasn't up to it health-wise and thought the program
needed some new blood. And I can use the extra money. I'm also one of the junior
class sponsors, and no one else was willing to be in charge of promoting the maga-
zine sales for the prom fund-raiser, so I said I'd do it."

"Wow, where was I when all this was going on? You know, Carina, it's OK to
come and talk to me about these additional responsibilities and whether or not you
should be taking them on. Between you and me, Josh Simmons should not have
offered you speech work in the way he did; seems to me like he 'guilted' you into
taking this on. And as for the other situation, well, it makes me want to shake my

finger at some of my elder colleagues. They should know better than to drop such a huge project on a new teacher."

"Oh, Melinda. You've been so great and so helpful to me with all my classroom management and planning questions. I just didn't think it was fair to keep coming to you to complain about things I took on without really thinking them through. And I don't seem to able to say no to Mr. Simmons, and I can't stand that the kids don't have people more enthusiastic about helping them with their fund-raiser. I was so organized in college!"

Melinda smiled. "You weren't juggling quite so many roles in college. Look, you need to go home, take a little breather, and then grade some more papers . . . but don't stay up all night. Hand papers back to the kids in your first through third hours, try to use your prep for nothing but grading, and if you still don't get finished, apologize profusely to sixth hour and tell them they'll get them the following day. And you and I are definitely meeting tomorrow when I get back from my presentation so we can talk through some strategies for saying no in a professional way."

Carina's situation is one many of us remember, and not too fondly. Most of us have those horror stories of having projects, extracurricular activities, and sponsorships dropped on us at the last minute with the expectation that we would do it all with grace and good humor. In addition, many beginning teachers live at sustenance levels their first few years in the profession; when extracurricular responsibilities come with monies, they may be more difficult for new educators to ignore.

Mentors need to be especially vigilant in this area; the reality is that novice teachers typically don't have the confidence or the professional maturity to say no to an administrator or to a colleague they consider their superior. Melinda's comment about the principal and senior colleagues was an honest one. Furthermore, it may help Carina realize that administrators and other colleagues do not always offer "opportunities" based on merit but on expediency. Melinda also offers sensible "take a breather" advice to Carina. Yes, Carina has dug herself into a hole, but it is not one from which she can't emerge triumphantly. In apologizing to her students, she will show them that, like them, she is not perfect. She will have to work to restore their faith in the promises she makes, but this situation will also help her evaluate more thoroughly what promises she can and cannot make to students regarding assessments and other issues. In addition, Melinda can help Carina develop a plan for handling her new extracurricular activities.

Melinda may also use this as an opportunity to share with her administrator what she has learned as a mentor about situations outside content pedagogy. In this way, Melinda provides a professional service to beginning teachers like Carina and those who come later, and she offers a subtle reminder to her administrator about positive practices in working with beginning teachers.

Personal Versus Professional Life

In methods courses, professors often warn preservice teachers that their personal lives will take a backseat to their professional lives during the student teaching experience, and that it will only get worse during their first year of teaching. Although this is true to varying degrees for all new educators, the inability to balance personal versus professional life can take on frightening dimensions all too quickly, as we see in the following example.

Marge was increasingly worried about her mentee, Karla. Karla, a second-year teacher, had experienced a wonderful first year in the classroom and had been enthusiastic about returning for a second year. When Karla found out in late September that she was having a baby, her twenty-eight third graders celebrated with her. But then the problems began. The pregnancy, Karla's third, was not an easy one, and she missed a number of days of school in both her first and second trimesters. Jack, Karla's husband, was laid off from his job because of the downturn in the economy. And Karla's mother, who had been planning an extended visit with her daughter's family to help with the daily routine of the household, had a change of plans and postponed her trip until closer to Karla's due date.

Karla was not getting a reprieve at school, either. Six of her twenty-eight students were ESL, five had Attention-Deficit/Hyperactivity Disorder (ADHD), and the class in general was a rowdy one. Two parents were critical of everything she did in the classroom, and they spent a great deal of time observing Karla and her students. Karla had no qualms about having the two mothers watch her as a teacher, but she found that their presence disrupted classroom routines, especially after one began to ask her questions about an activity the students were doing while they were doing it. In addition, Karla had her usual lunch and playground duties as well as two service committees, one for which she was chair.

At first, Karla shared many of her frustrations with Marge and felt better because of Marge's support. But as the semester and the pregnancy wore on, she became more distant and less able to deal with all the demands on her time. Once, as Marge was nearing Karla's door, she heard the class before she saw them. Stopping in the doorway, Marge saw Karla at her desk, absently staring out the window while the kids surged around the room in excited bunches. At the end of the day, Marge went back to Karla's room to find out what had been going on.

"I can't do this anymore, Marge," said Karla. "I'm exhausted all the time; I couldn't care less about writing lesson plans, much less teaching them. I'm sick of those two women questioning everything I do. You don't know how I'd like to just walk out this door and never come back."

"Karla, I know things are rough right now, but in a couple of months, you'll be at home with the baby and then you'll have the summer. And I know you'll want to come back and teach next year; you loved this so much last year."

"I don't love it now." Karla looked at her mentor as her eyes clouded over with tears. "My life is a mess. Jack finally got some part-time work, but he's not doing anything at home. And Bobby and Jenny [Karla's other children] have been so demanding lately; I think they already sense how much of my time the new baby will take. I know I can't quit this job; we have to have the insurance. But I just don't have the energy, and Mr. Fredley [the principal] came in three days ago and gave me a terrible evaluation; he went over it with me this morning during recess, and after that, I was just too numb to care about the rest of the day. And that's what you saw."

For mentors, a situation like Karla's can be extremely difficult. Marge's first reaction is sympathy for Karla's predicament; her second is practical: how she can sustain Karla's professional persona until her maternity leave begins. As a friend, Marge may be able to help Karla in her personal life by offering to help with household chores or cooking, but many mentors do not necessarily work with their mentees outside the school day. In her capacity as mentor, Marge needs to help Karla find ways to deal with the stress at school so that she can function effectively as a teacher for herself and her students.

If Marge is also a third-grade teacher, she might look for ways to team with Karla during this difficult time to the benefit of both sets of students and teachers. She could also encourage Karla to speak more openly with the principal as part of a three-way dialogue so that Mr. Fredley would have a better sense of the difficulties Karla is facing. They could also use this as an opportunity to ask for the principal's advice on how to deal with the very attentive and often distracting parents in Karla's classroom.

The important factor to keep in mind for the mentor working with someone who is having difficulty balancing personal and professional responsibilities is helping that person look critically at how the two can mesh rather than how they pull at each other. Mentors who can offer practical advice on how to juggle the personal and professional, how to prioritize for the short term as well as the long term, and/or when to look for help when the balancing act is not working can help decrease the high numbers of teachers leaving the profession.

Struggling Student Teachers

Tess felt as if the walls were closing in on her . . . again. It was 3 A.M. and she was still planning her lessons for the following day. In fact, this was the third night in a row she had stayed up this late planning for the next day. And if the last two mornings were any indication of how effective that late-night planning was, she was going to be in big trouble when she got to school. Nothing that she planned seemed to work with these kids, and she knew her mentor, Janisa, was unhappy with her work. As much as she wanted to blame Janisa, her university supervisor, Clark, for placing her at this school, or the kids for simply being in the class, she knew the fault lay with her. At the beginning of the semester, she had planned for the entire week, listened attentively to Janisa's suggestions for improvement, and looked forward to Clark's observation. But when she actually got up to teach, nothing seemed to go as planned. She got nervous and lost her place in the lesson or she failed to give the students some vital piece of information necessary for them to finish an assignment. And they didn't listen to her very well, which she found frustrating; she often responded to what she saw as their lack of respect by yelling at them, which only seemed to egg them on.

As the weeks had gone by, Tess had rebelled against what she considered the students' lack of interest by not planning as much or as thoroughly as she had in the beginning. When Janisa had commented on the lack of a lesson plan, Tess had airily replied that if super planning didn't keep the kids involved, maybe "winging it" was a better response. When Clark showed up later in the afternoon, Tess wasn't surprised. In the ensuing meeting, Clark, Tess, and Janisa talked honestly about Tess's strengths and weaknesses, her attitudes toward students, her growing antipathy toward teaching in general, and the support she had received from Janisa and the university. When Clark left that afternoon, he noted that it was Tess and Tess alone who had to decide the future of her student teaching. Tess spent a long week-end considering the pros and cons of continuing with a career in education, and on Monday morning, told Clark and Janisa that she wanted to stick it out.

One option for mentors with struggling student teachers is to work with the university supervisor in creating a contract for improvement. Most universities have these types of plans in place to support student teachers and their mentors when problems seem especially difficult or consistent. (See the sample at the end of this chapter.)

Assisting Struggling Early-Career Teachers

Teachers in their first two or three years of teaching, depending upon the state, are assigned probation status. This period determines whether the teacher remains in the profession, essentially because at the end of those two or three years, schools or states typically award some type of formal or informal tenure.

Almost all studies suggest that mentoring and evaluation should not be mixed and that a colleague other than the department chair should be the mentor (Bey and Holmes 1992; Darling-Hammond 1994; Levine 1992). Beginning teachers should feel that their conversations with their mentors are confidential. Administrators should be the ones conducting formal evaluations of the beginning teacher. Mentors should not be part of the evaluation process but can assist their colleagues in preparing for pre-observation conferences, observations, and post-observation conferences. By talking through the evaluative process, struggling teachers may be better able to enumerate their successes and describe to their mentors how they are working toward other goals.

Most beginners struggle during their initial years. Mentors often encourage beginners not to give up on teaching for at least two years, because the second year is usually much easier than the first. They usually just need to reinforce the beginner's successes.

In some cases, mentors can help beginning teachers determine whether teaching is their ideal career path. In the scenario to follow, Zarina and Tom discuss Tom's future as a teacher.

Zarina: What did you want to talk about, Tom?

Tom: Well, I'm halfway through my second year, but teaching just isn't what I expected. I'm not happy and I don't think I'm necessarily doing right by my students.

Zarina: Has something new happened since the last time we talked?

Tom: Well, I'm really getting tired of feeling like I work harder than all of my friends. They have nine-to-five jobs, and they don't have to bring home any work at night. I usually feel like I should be bringing work every night, but I find myself going out with friends, not preparing for school, and then feeling guilty, but probably not guilty enough, when the next day is a disaster.

Zarina: So you've stopped trying to find a balance between your personal and your professional life?

Tom: Yeah, and that's not all. I don't have much patience with the students anymore. I get mad and yell at them . . . a lot. And I haven't been getting very good evaluations from Mrs. Bailey, and I'm guessing that she isn't going to be too excited about renewing my contract. Plus, she's still upset that I blew up at Billy's dad in front of other parents and faculty members.

Zarina: Well, it wasn't your finest moment.

Tom: Nope.

Zarina: So, Tom, are you trying to tell me that you don't think you want to stay in teaching?

Tom: I am contemplating leaving; I'm just not sure. I still have the occasional day when I think I could be an effective teacher.

Zarina: OK, then why don't you try this: Make one list of what you like about teaching and then compare it with the second list you'll make, showing what you don't like. It should be fairly clear from that where you're leaning.

Tom: And when I've done that?

Zarina: Maybe you could brainstorm other careers you're considering, list their pros and cons, and compare that list with your teaching list.

Tom: Well, it's worth a try. Thanks for listening. I'll probably give you a call in a few days to talk through this a bit more.

The underlying reality throughout this situation is that there are, on occasion, people who really are not cut out to be teachers. While it is always difficult to tell people who have spent a number of years preparing to teach that they are not suited to the profession, all of us must be vigilant regarding unsuccessful classroom teachers. Our K–12 students deserve solid teaching, and as members of the same professional community, we need to support each other to the point where we realize that a member of that community cannot or will not make the necessary changes to their teaching to be success-ful. At that point, we need to encourage, in the most positive manner possi-ble, that person to leave the profession.

Summary

Beginning teachers struggle for numerous reasons. This chapter focuses on those teachers whose struggles are the most difficult. Mentors especially need to be aware of teachers who lack confidence, knowledge, or skills. Mentors also need to be cognizant of problematic areas such as inadequate planning or management issues that are not easily rectified. Pressures from parents and/or administrators may cause further complications. Often, beginning teachers feel overwhelmed by their responsibilities and may become con-flicted when attempting to separate their personal and professional lives. Individuals with alternative licensure who are simultaneously taking classes and teaching full time may be especially at-risk in a number of the areas dis-cussed here.

At-risk beginning teachers do not necessarily need to stop teaching. As is evident throughout this chapter, wise and consistent mentoring can effec-tively support new educators through the rough spots. However, we must face the reality that some people will not be successful in the classroom and will quit teaching. As difficult as that may be, it is better that unsuccessful people leave the classroom than to become negative influences in students' lives. As members of the same community, we want dedicated, caring educa-tors in the teaching profession.

Sample Student Teaching Contract for Remediation Plan

To become an effective teacher at the designated student teaching placement, the student teacher _____

needs to make adjustment in the following checked areas:

__ Arrive at school at the designated time.

__ Maintain few or no additional absences.

__ Establish and use effective classroom management strategies.

__ Interact with students in an engaging, professional manner.

__ Plan more thoroughly.

__ Share written lesson plans in advance with the cooperating teacher.

__ E-mail or postal mail the lesson plans to the university supervisor following the conference with the cooperating teacher.

__ Prepare handouts and assessments more thoroughly.

__ Assess and return student work promptly.

__ Other. Please specify: _____

Teaching strategies to achieve these skills:

Desired outcomes:

Proposed time line:

Result

__ Satisfactory progress

__ Unsatisfactory progress

   __ additional student teaching experience required

   __ not receiving state licensure

Student teacher:_____ Date:_____

Cooperating teacher:_____ Date:_____

University supervisor:_____ Date:_____

Thinking Outside the Box: Using Technology to Support Mentoring

When I look back over my career, I suppose one regret is that I wasn't able to share more of what worked [for me in the classroom] and what didn't work with those just coming into the field. I know that when I got to go to conferences, it was people telling their success stories that really got me excited about leaving the conference and going back home to work with my students. We really never took the time to do that at my school; we used that favorite comment "We're too busy." But I wish we had been more able to talk.

Myrna, retired teacher

Myrna's lament is one to which many of us can relate. As teachers, we all have much to share and little time to do so. But if we are chosen to act as mentors, we must find the opportunity to support beginning teachers sufficiently. On occasion, some of us are asked to mentor colleagues in unique situations: those teaching overseas or in schools some physical distance away. In addition, there is the important mentoring needed to support colleagues who have made a lifelong commitment to teaching but may not have easy access to newer materials or current teaching trends that could positively affect their classrooms.

This chapter highlights mentoring facilitated through technology such as e-mail and listservs. We focus specifically on the mentoring of student teachers overseas or at a site a lengthy physical distance from their university supervisor. The final section of this chapter provides a number of professional organizations' Web sites that include chat rooms and/or listservs that may supply additional options for those teachers who do not have mentoring close at hand.

Using Listservs for Teachers and Student Teachers

Teaching overseas. Teaching more than 300 miles away from the university. When student teachers are found in these situations, it is usually because, for any number of reasons they have requested an unusual placement. However, they can provide severe headaches for university mentors asked to keep track of students they may not be able to see easily or who ask to come to campus for bimonthly student teaching seminar meetings.

In this chapter, we look at a way to mentor "long distance." When student teachers are placed overseas or at a considerable distance from the university for their student teaching experience, university supervisors often are, because of space, time, and financial considerations, constrained to one main observation during the semester. This observation, typically occurring during the middle of the student teaching experience, may include time for two or three classroom observations, but provide little opportunity for the supervisor to see significant changes in the quality of teaching. With those who are teaching in state but a long distance away and who are therefore unable to come to campus for seminar meetings, the content specialist working with the students may want to help them stay in touch with colleagues. In cases like these, e-mail mentoring can provide crucial links both pre- and post-observation.

Setting up the Experience

In an informal discussion of how students felt about student teaching overseas, Thalia shared the following with her university supervisor:

> *I'm excited and nervous about student teaching overseas. I already feel that student teaching is a big, nerve-wracking, exciting adventure and I can't wait to start. And teaching in Europe will just add to the adventure. But I am a little worried about what might go wrong. You [the university supervisor] will be a long ways away and I've heard the horror stories about bad cooperating teachers*

and the things that go wrong. I worry if e-mail is "fast" enough for dealing with the problems.

Surveys distributed to both student and mentor teachers before the field-work experience can provide the university supervisor important information about what those involved in the mentoring relationship expect from the experience, each other, principals, the university supervisor, and themselves. (A sample survey for a mentor teacher and for a beginning teacher can be found in Appendix B.)

These surveys can then be used by the university mentor to set a baseline for expectations about interactions with both student and mentor teacher, which is important if the supervisor does not know either of the teachers well. In Thalia's survey answers, she notes that she is looking for "wise mentoring," "suggestions without demands," "support for trying new things and/or being challenged to grow." From principals and university supervisors, Thalia expects much of the same. And from herself, she expects "hard work, organization, enthusiasm for my content and my students."

The surveys we considered revealed that the best mentors were looking for student teachers who were "willing to listen" and "try a variety of approaches." All wanted to see "independence in actions," "creativity," "dedication," and "a high level of professionalism." From themselves as mentors, most expressed a desire to "be supportive and patient as necessary as she works through teaching issues, problems."

These insights from all involved give university supervisors some clues as to how the relationship may develop between the student and mentor teacher. However, by themselves these are no guarantee, even when the answers are similar. Therefore, for the supervisor who would like to continue the conversation, two listservs, one for students and one for mentors, may be the best way to keep communication open and vital among participants. These can be used before the actual observation period and again when the supervisor has returned to the university to continue the conversations begun and then extended during the actual observations.

The Student Listserv

A listserv for student teachers is a sensible approach to student teacher support, whether the student teacher is in the same locale as the supervisor or

2,000 miles away. The fact is that student teachers may feel some of the same isolation in the classroom that their mentor teachers do, and for students used to chatting with classmates, the listserv may help alleviate some of their "withdrawal" from the university support system. In this section, we consider how the student listserv can be used to

- set expectations and respond to queries,
- share critical incident reports, and
- maintain expectations after on-site visits.

Setting Expectations and Responding to Queries

Whenever one is using a listserv to aid in student teaching fieldwork experiences, baseline expectations must be set to maximize the value of the listserv interchanges. Student teachers placed overseas should be asked to respond to listserv messages from the university supervisor and/or their overseas colleagues at least four times a week, and more often if possible. The supervisor can also encourage the beginning teachers to ask and respond to questions in the most honest manner possible since the listserv will, in essence, belong to the students and their supervisor. There must be the understanding that the mentor teacher will not be privy to the student listserv and that the students will not see conversations on the mentor listserv. Privacy issues are pragmatic ones. For students who are in difficult situations, the need to vent honestly, share concerns, and voice disapproval of the mentor may be more necessary when the university supervisor is more than a phone call away. Differences in time zones as well as the cost of long-distance telephone bills make phone calls a less convenient means of conferring.

Critical Incident Reports However, the listserv should not be a place where chatting is the only form of communication. Critical incident reports can be required on a regular basis, and the other student teachers can be asked to respond to the original report with similar experiences and how they were handled or with additional questions that stem from their consideration of the incident itself. Critical incident reports are, essentially, one-page, single-spaced accounts of something that happened in the classroom that could be questioned in terms of how it was handled. In the following example from Kendra, we watch her use the events of September 11, 2001, to create a teachable moment and, accordingly, a classroom management quandary that she would benefit from greatly.

Incident Report on Period Four World History—Kendra Kelly

The first day that I took over fourth-period world history was quite a learning experience. Due to the tragic events that occurred on September 11, I decided to postpone my lesson on the Indus civilization and instead do a lesson on terrorism. Because of the unique situation of the students, I had felt that it was important to provide them with the opportunity to voice their opinions and concerns. I began the lesson by having students write a response to the following quote: "I hate them; not for their race, not for their brutality, I hate them because they've left us no way out." Initially I did not tell them the author of the quote (Michael Collins—Irish revolutionary) because I wanted them to respond to the words and not the man.

The use of the quote was extremely effective in drawing out the students' reactions, and the first forty minutes of the discussion went very well. The students were very engaged, passionate, and eager to have their opinion heard. However, as the discussion grew in intensity, several students started discussing the issues among themselves rather than waiting until they "had the floor" to share their thoughts. Consequently, the noise level began to rise above an acceptable level. My first response was to remind the students to respect one another by not talking over one another. This technique was effective for about five to ten minutes, and then I would have to address the noise level again. After reminding several students individually, I changed tactics and told the class collectively that they would have the "privilege" of remaining with me after the bell rang. The strategy worked in that the noise level remained at an acceptable level, but I felt that I had overreacted.

Upon reflection, I believe that I could have handled the situation differently. First of all, I should have stated my expectations for the format of the discussion at the beginning of class. Second, when I noticed the students beginning to discuss the issue among themselves, I could have broken the class into smaller discussion groups so that everyone would have the opportunity to be heard.

Overall the class went well and the discussion was positive and productive. I will definitely have more class discussions, but in the future I will provide the students with more of a structure in which to discuss their views. I don't want any student to feel that they did not have the chance to be heard.

In this reflection, the student teacher is confronted by a management issue with which she has not previously dealt. First, she explains the situation and the problem. Then she discusses how it was actually handled and the repercussions. Finally, she discusses why, on reflection, she would have handled the problem differently, in a way that might have had a more satisfactory outcome.

Management issues surfacing in critical incident reports usually happen a great deal in the beginning of the semester. Beginning teachers are usually relieved to find out that their colleagues are having many of the same problems. In this case, the critical incident helped the "comrades in pain" bond (as another student teacher, Alicia, put it) and provided them the opportunity to commiserate, share ideas, and practice the teacher literacy discussed earlier in this chapter. Unit planning, parent/teacher issues, and administrative problems become more prevalent topics as the semester continues.

Maintaining Expectations When the university supervisor arrives at the off-campus destination, the information generated through the listserv discussions may help provide a baseline for what to expect during the visit. With an overseas student teaching situation, the supervisor typically sees four to six students in schools that may be anywhere from one to four hours away from one another; in that circumstance, two to three class observations may be the norm. Even when the supervisor can split his or her time between schools or even between the student teachers, a one-week separation between observations may not provide enough time for young teachers to show professional growth. Thus, these observations become a general standard by which the supervisor may have to judge performance at the time of the visit as well as toward the end of the semester. Consequently, the listservs remain important after the university supervisor carries out the observation, especially for those placed overseas, as the way to share or explain how the supervisor's comments have been used in the classroom. These updates are absolutely necessary if the supervisor is going to continue supporting the students' growth in the classroom.

Teacher Listservs

A listserv for teacher mentors may also be a good idea, and not just for sharing suggestions about mentoring student teachers. The teacher listserv can serve the same purpose as the student teacher listserv in terms of bringing people together, helping the mentor teachers understand university or supervisor expectations, and clarifying post-observation visit interactions. Mentors can commiserate with each other on problems they're having with their student teachers. However, they may also use this kind of forum to exchange information on texts that could be of use to others, discuss trends in the field that affect all of them, or share Web sites or project ideas. It should be noted, though, that university supervisors usually can't require mentors to take part in a listserv. Encouraging interactions is the most promising approach, and if the supervisor can offer information on issues or trends of interest to the teachers with whom he or she is working, the listserv may illustrate its own importance quickly.

Greetings:

Two questions this morning, possibly unrelated. Does the university have a policy on sharing student teachers with another teacher? My student teacher says that in her department, she isn't supposed to work with more than one teacher, but I know that at the two DoDDS [Department of Defense] schools at which I've worked, we've routinely shared. And I think I have a potentially wonderful opportunity for Alicia if I can switch her out for one class a day.

Second, my student teacher is very professional, which I appreciate immensely, but very shy when it's just the two of us. I've been very open with her . . . am I pushing too hard? My last student teacher was so friendly, and I'm wondering if I got spoiled a bit with her. We still correspond.

Beth

Cheers, all:

I do know that the university doesn't encourage more than two teachers to a student teacher, but they don't outlaw it. And Jack [the DoDDS liaison at the university] knows that sometimes it's hard to not split up the student teaching experience. So I'd recommend you talk to Jean, or Jean, when you get this, let us know how you feel about it since you're the supervisor.

As to the other, I think you should consider yourself lucky that the professional is so well in place. She'll have sixteen weeks to loosen up on the other. And I don't think it has anything to do with you. When student teachers come to us, they either feel the need to bond quickly because they're so far from home, or they feel they really need to prove their professionalism because they're so far away from home. I've noticed that they all loosen up fairly quickly because they come to

*understand that we're a small, tight-knit community here on and around the
base.*

    Craig

*P.S. Does anyone know if there are any new young adult books dealing with boys
in emotional crisis?*

Hi, Beth and others:

    *I'm the "department" that doesn't recommend splitting because we've had so
many bad experiences with it here in the States. But I am willing to have my
mind changed on this concerning DoDDS situations because I have heard from
Jack and others that flexibility takes on even greater meaning for all of you. So
Beth, please feel free to share.*

    *As to the professionalism, I'd have to agree with Craig; he summed that up
well.*

    *And yes, Craig, I do have a couple of books in which you might be interested.
One is Paul Fleischman's* Whirligig, *about a young man who kills a young
woman who had been an inspiration to others; her mother requests that he go
around the country making and placing whirligigs in her memory. Another good
choice is Nancy Werlin's* The Killer's Cousin, *about a boy who may or may not
have murdered his girlfriend and the repercussions of that for him and his family.
Finally, Chris Crutcher's newest book* Whale Talk *has an amazing cast of "misfits" who make readers reconsider their own biases about a number of issues. All
are great reads.*

    Jean

As with the student listserv, the importance of continuing the talk after
observations is also important, although some situations may call for a more
private approach: the direct e-mail.

E-mail

Having consistent individual e-mails with students and mentors should be
considered a must for university supervisors. Encouraging conversation may
help students feel more comfortable sharing their triumphs and challenges in
the classroom. Writing directly before the first visit to the mentors may help
clarify university expectations of what the supervisor needs to see the student teacher "doing" during the observations. Inevitably, the e-mail may also
have to be used for "cries for help."

Dear Dr. B,

I have written this letter a million times in my head, but I'm still not sure if I've got it right. This e-mail is not a personal attack on Ms. C; it is simply a solicitation for advice. The other student teachers have advised me to be brutally honest, so I will. Ms. C [mentor teacher] is one of those teachers who has been at the school for 20-some years and she does things HER way, because she can. She is totally eccentric, wildly creative, and most of all "the queen of her own little world." I have no problem with this; we actually get along quite well. What I struggle with is a lack of communication from her. I am not getting the feedback from her I desire. I'll receive a "that went fine" or "that was great" and she appreciates me, but never offers any constructive criticism on my lessons, and criticizes me in conversation with other student teachers. At the end of the day, I am here to learn how to teach and Ms. C does not appear to have the time or inclination to mentor me. Ms. C didn't want a student teacher and unfortunately I don't think she knows how to because I am walking on eggshells. I have been warned not to be "too good" or become "too popular with the students" because then Ms. C will no longer like me. We never sit down and plan because she is always too busy running in ten directions at once. Please try to understand my situation— any feedback/advice you can offer would be greatly appreciated. I am planning to sit down with Ms. C and express my concerns to her Monday, so I will give you a full update. Other teachers have told me that she has "turned" on student teachers before.

Furthermore, I am definitely learning about the politics within a school. I feel like I am caught in a battle zone because I have had to look to the other English teachers for guidance, an action she resents. Ms. C has not turned the class over to me yet . . . perhaps it is because she is uncomfortable relinquishing control. I am being respectful of her classroom (I am a guest within); however, I feel like I am treated more like a classroom aide than a student teacher. I feel that you should know I am being limited in my abilities.

Cherie

Hi, Cherie:

Thanks for the info. I can tell you that in my e-mails with Ms. C, she has said that you are fabulous. And because I'm saving all of the e-mails, she can't take that back no matter what happens! Seriously, I am sorry to hear that you're being so limited. She does know what the university expectations are concerning the amount of time you need to be planning for and in front of the class. You might remind her that I will be arriving October 1 and will be expecting to watch you teach on October 1 or October 2. Ideally, that will force the issue to some degree so that she will let you take over more of the day.

If you're still not doing much by the 1st, then when I sit down with you and Ms. C to discuss my first observation, we will talk honestly about why you need to be doing more planning for and taking over classes. I will also ask her whether there are concerns she has that she simply has not been willing to share with you face to face or with me by e-mail. I will be respectful of her position, of course, but the reality is that you have to have the opportunity to teach during student teaching so that when you come back to the states, you're ready to go into a classroom.

More soon! Dr. B

In this set of e-mails, we see how important it is for the student to have a safe place to vent to one of the people who may actually be able to facilitate change. Obviously, Cherie had already spoken with her colleagues about the situation, and when the university supervisor finally arrived in Europe, she found out that the other teachers in the department had taken it upon themselves to mentor Cherie in terms of the politics of the situation. Nevertheless, her e-mail to the supervisor was important because she had taken courses with the supervisor and the supervisor knew her background, both professionally and personally. In that sense, the supervisor was well aware of Cherie's capabilities in the classroom and knew her well enough to know whether she was exaggerating in her account of the situation. The supervisor's response, while professional, also offered Cherie reassurance that her concerns were taken seriously and that she would troubleshoot the situation when all three of us could meet together.

Ideally, e-mails can also be an opportunity to share successes and/or humorous situations that end well. Thalia seemed to have both in the following e-mail:

Dr. B,

How's this for an incident report . . .

I was about to do an active viewing of two different versions of Julius Caesar. *If you recall from your visit, the TV is propped up on the wall and sits on a small metal platform above the computer. Because of the size of the TV in relation to the stability of the platform it sits on, the TV can be a bit wobbly. Well, I had finished my motivation, and the students were all set to start the viewing. I reached up to turn the TV on, and pushed the "power" button just a little too hard. The TV wobbled and fell from its platform . . . onto me. Two students rushed to help move the fallen TV out of the way. I sent a third student to the office to tell them what had happened. I remembered that Kendra's classroom was empty this class period and removed the class from this exciting environment into her class to try to watch the video in there. The class goes into Kendra's room, sit down, and of course, I can't get the VCR to work.*

Now, I realize that the class is extremely riled up. It's last period, the TV has fallen on their student teacher, we've moved classrooms, and VCRs are not my friends. So, I turn to the class and give them a choice:

(1) We return to my classroom, finish Act V by acting it out, which means that we finish JC. Then, the next class period they can spend the majority of the period working on their final projects.

or

(2) We return to my classroom and use the remainder of the time working on JC projects and finish Act V the next class period.

We ended up with choice No. 2. I'm glad of this because I knew that after so much excitement, I would have to fight to get the class quiet enough to read, act, and concentrate on JC. Amazingly, though, they did work very diligently on their projects for the remainder of the period. I have to say that in my troubleshooting, I never planned for the TV's tumbling down. My backup plan for if the VCR/TV didn't work was simply that we would act out the play. However, the tumbling TV caused a different atmosphere in the classroom, and I chose to let the students continue with their energy as they worked in groups instead of trying to control it.

I think that the situation was handled pretty well. If I had to guess, I think I lost about ten minutes' time in the class. I am sure that it could have been handled better, but I have to admit that I don't think I was exactly altogether in my own mind. I did my best to think quickly and hope that my actions weren't too rash. By the way, this happened in my Period 6 sophomore class . . . the "high-energy class" that you observed. They were great. :)

Quite the day, Thalia

Thalia's e-mail is a good example of a post-observation report. Because the university supervisor has already completed her on-site observations of the student teacher, Thalia's tone is more casual and assumes a certain level of understanding on the part of her university mentor. She knows that "Dr. B." knows her classroom setup, her lesson setup, the layout of the school, and the class with which she's working. Thalia also is able to express what she's learned through her education courses as well as student teaching concerning how to react to those moments not planned for in the lesson.

The teachers also used the e-mail to share positive and/or worrisome situations as merited. The following came from Cherie's second mentor teacher, who also happened to be co-mentoring Kendra.

> *Greetings!*
>
> *Haven't been in touch for a while so I thought I'd give you some status updates. Cherie has been teaching my senior language arts classes for the past several weeks. She is continually getting more and more confidence, has planned well, and is performing at a sustained level of excellence. The students, leery at first, adore her even if she is "teachin' lousy vocabulary"! Cherie selects five words every other day, and when the kids see her they have to use the words in her presence (in sentences). It has really made a difference in everyday usage and the middle-schoolers keep staring at the seniors, impressed with their $25 words. One of the students came in the other day to say that she and her mother had a knock-down, drag-out fight. She used at least seven of her vocabulary words in the course of her argument. She wanted us to know that her mother said, "Great! Now she isn't just a smartass, she's actually smart!"*
>
> *Kendra has outdone herself with the three-school debate. Sharon, her other mentor, thinks that Kendra walks on water! She did the initial planning, lunch arrangements, agenda, debate topics, scoring, and final selection for our school's representatives. I don't know what my history classes are going to do when she leaves! She had a parent come into school today and insist on talking to her because his daughter did well only in her class. He wanted to meet the teacher and find out what techniques she was using to motivate Michelle, his daughter, to get her so excited about history. I am fortunate to have two wonderful kids that will make outstanding teachers. Thanks for sending top quality kids.*
>
> *Ken*

Ken's e-mail is a strong example of a good mentoring e-mail. Within a few well-written paragraphs, he articulates to the university supervisor how the teaching experiences are working for the two student teachers he is mentoring. He quickly reestablishes for the absent supervisor the strengths of the beginning teachers, then provides an anecdote that underscores the effectiveness of each one. His last comments are an added bonus for any university supervisor, but on a pragmatic level, may also help university programs understand what they are doing well in teacher preparation.

Throughout these examples, it becomes clear that e-mails and listservs can help mitigate the sense of isolation for student teachers and mentors, especially when they do not have consistent access to the university supervisor or other colleagues. Listservs should also be considered if one is at a university where a number of students are placed out of state yet have expressed an interest in staying in touch with colleagues at the university. Although we would hate for face-to-face conversations to ever be phased out of the mentor relationship, we see this approach as a sensible support system when consistent observations are not an option.

Continuing the Conversation: Mentoring and Supporting Veteran Teachers

Obviously, most of our focus in this text is the mentoring of beginning teachers. However, we also see a need for supporting those veteran teachers who teach in remote and isolated areas that make it difficult for them to attend conferences, take additional coursework, or find colleagues with whom to sit and talk. Recent Internet growth and the awareness in educational circles that technology provides us with new options for learning allow us to consider new ways to mentor and support those of us who have been in the profession for more than five years.

As noted earlier, e-mail and listservs for teachers can be a great way to keep collegial conversation alive. At universities with student affiliates of national associations, alumni listservs provide consistent opportunities for outreach and conversation among graduates. Professional organizations have created much of the same. (See Appendix A for a list of organizations that have developed listservs and chat rooms for their memberships.)

Not only do these listservs provide opportunities for colleagues to share, but the organizations behind them also provide sites on a variety of educational issues and/or content and pedagogical concerns of use to teachers.

Summary

Technology should be considered a tool that can aid in the mentoring process. Although face-to-face mentoring will always be the best way to work with colleagues, mentoring by computer can be a useful support in beginning the conversation and supporting it in a variety of situations. That mentoring is possible through e-mail and the information can be conveyed quickly across distance are two of the most important aspects of Internet communication for teachers. The nature of the support necessary among mentors and beginning teachers that could easily be lost across distances can be reestablished and maintained efficiently through Internet exchanges. By the nature of our profession, teachers must be strong communicators. The Internet allows us to be that in almost any situation.

Internet Resources for Mentors and Beginning Teachers

The following Web addresses provide listservs and chat rooms that teachers from a variety of disciplines may find useful. These lists are by no means exhaustive, but may provide a starting point for any number of professional conversations.

Arts Education

National Art Education Association (NAEA). www.naea-reston.org/

Bilingual Education

California Association for Bilingual Education (CABE).
   www.bilingualeducation.org/

National Association for Bilingual Education (NABE). www.nabe.org/

Educational Technology

The Education Coalition—Distributed Learning Systems and Services.
   www.tecweb.org/index.html

International Technology Education Association. www.iteawww.org/

English Education

The National Council of Teachers of English. www.ncte.org/lists/

The International Reading Association.
   www.reading.org/advocacy/govrel_listserv.html

The Great Books Foundation. www.greatbooks.org/participate/index.shtml

National Institute for Literacy. www.nifl.gov/

History/Social Studies Education

National Council for the Social Studies.
www.socialstudies.org/links/listserv.html

The Organization of History Teachers. users.rcn.com/viceroy1/OHT.htm

The National Council of Economic Education. www.ncee.net/

Mathematics

Association of Teachers of Mathematics. www.atm.org.uk/

National Council of Teachers of Mathematics. www.nctm.org/

National Council of Supervisors of Mathematics.
www.nscmonline.org/OtherResources/listserv.html

Modern Languages

American Association of Teachers of French. frenchteachers.org/redirect.htm

American Association of Teachers of German. www.aatg.org/

American Association of Teachers of Spanish & Portuguese. www.aatsp.org/

American Council on the Teaching of Foreign Languages. www.actfl.org/

Computer Assisted Language Instruction Consortium. calico.org/

National Network for Early Language Learning (NNELL).
www.educ.iastate.edu/nnell

Music Education

The National Association for Music Education.
www.menc.org/networks/genmus/openforum/wwwboard.htm

The Kennedy Center Arts Edge. artsedge.kennedy-center.org/teaching-materials/ideaexch/artsedge.html

Physical Education

National High School Coaches Association. www.nhsca.com/

National High School Athletic Coaches Association. www.hscoaches.org/

Science Education

National Association of Biology Teachers. www.nabt.org/

National Center for Improving Student Learning and Achievement in Mathematics and Science. www.wcer.wisc.edu/NCISLA/mailing/index.html

National Science Teachers Association. www.nsta.org/main/forum/

The Science Center. www.science-education.org/egi-bin/mesg.cgi

American Association of Physics Teachers. www.aapt.org/

Talented and Gifted Education

Center for Gifted Education. www.apa.org/ed/cgeplistserv.html

Professional Training for Teachers of the Gifted and Talented. www5.kidsource.com/forums

California Association for the Gifted. www.cagifted.org/discuss.htm

Council for Exceptional Children. www.cec.sped.org/

National Association for Gifted Children. www.nagc.org/

Sample Mentoring Questionnaires

Mentoring Questionnaire for Mentor Teachers

1. Define a mentor.

2. Describe your teaching style and your educational philosophy.

3. What were your experiences as a student teacher? As a first-year teacher?

4. What kind of teachers mentored you during your early years in the profession and how did they mentor you?

5. As you have moved into more senior positions, what mentoring/suggestions have you offered others?

6. What do you expect beginning teachers/your student teacher to know as he/she comes into the profession, into this building, into your department?

7. What do you expect from yourself in terms of your mentoring a beginning teacher?

8. How do teachers in your building work with student teachers and first- and second-year teachers in general? For example, are they immediately put into a mentoring program? Are they assigned specific mentors?

9. Do you receive compensation for any of your mentoring?

10. (If working with a student teacher) What do you expect the university supervisor to do for you, for your student teacher, during this experience?

11. Other comments on necessary attributes for successful mentoring.

Mentoring Questionnaire for Beginning Teachers

1. Define a mentor.

2. Describe your teaching style and your educational philosophy.

3. What do you expect from this student teaching experience? or, As a first-year teacher, what do you think you will need from a mentor?

4. What do you think you can offer your mentor teacher? Or, what do you need to do to be successful in this situation?

5. What do you expect from your university supervisor in terms of mentor-ship? From the principal of this school?

6. What do you think you should know as a beginning teacher moving into the profession, into this building, into your department?

7. What is your biggest fear about this first semester/year of teaching?

8. Other comments.

Contributors

Susan Kimball has been teaching high school English for more than thirty years. She has obtained her National Board for Professional Teaching Standards, attended National Endowment for the Humanities Institutes, served as a facilitator for the Iowa Writing Project, published several teaching articles, and mentored countless teachers.

Robert Petrone taught middle and high school English in Colorado and New York. He is currently pursuing a Ph.D. in English education at Michigan State University. His research interests include approaches to teaching literature in secondary schools, social issues in the English classroom, canonization, and censorship.

Sandra Raymond teaches English education at Northern Arizona University, and she has also taught middle school in Flagstaff. She is currently working on her doctorate in curriculum and instruction, and her first novel. Her main area of research involves looking at best practices in writing instruction at the secondary level.

Sarah Brown Wessling has taught for five years, the last four at Johnston High School in Johnston, Iowa. She has completed her master's degree in literature at Iowa State University, has received the Future Leader in Education award from the Iowa Council of Teachers of English, and is actively involved in leadership in her school district.

References

Aragon, Steven, ed. 2000. "Beyond Access: Methods and Models for Increasing Retention and Learning Among Minority Students." *New Directions for Community Colleges, No. 112.* San Francisco: Jossey-Bass.

Atwell, Nancie. 1998. *In the Middle: New Understandings About Writing, Reading, and Learning.* Portsmouth, NH: Heinemann.

Beebe, Samuel J., and Patricia Margerison, 1995. "Teaching the Newest Members of the Family to Teach: Whose Responsibility?" *English Journal* 84, 2: 33–37.

Belenky, Mary Field, Blythe McVicker Clinchy, Nancy Rule Goldberger, and Jill Mattuck Tarule. 1986. *Women's Ways of Knowing: The Development of Self, Voice, and Mind.* New York: HarperCollins.

Bey, Theresa M., and C. Thomas Holmes, eds. 1992. *Mentoring: Contemporary Principles and Issues.* Reston, VA: Association of Teacher Educators.

Bloom, Benjamin S. 1964. *Taxonomy of Educational Objectives: Cognitive Domain.* New York: Longman.

Boreen, Jean, Mary K. Johnson, Donna Niday, and Joe Potts. 2000. *Mentoring Beginning Teachers: Guiding, Reflecting, Coaching.* Portland, ME: Stenhouse.

Britton, James, Tony Burgess, Nancy Martin, Alex McLeod, and Harold Rosen. 1975. *The Development of Writing Abilities (11–18).* London: McMillan Education.

Brookfield, Stephen D. 1987. *Developing Critical Thinkers: Challenging Adults to Explore Alternative Ways of Thinking and Acting.* San Francisco: Jossey-Bass.

Campbell, Dorothy M., Pamela Bondi Cignetti, Beverly J. Melenyzer, Diana Nettles, and Richard M. Wyman. 1997. *How to Develop a Professional Portfolio: A Manual for Teachers.* Needham, MA: Allyn and Bacon.

Canfield, John Y. 1990. *The Looking-Glass Self: An Examination of Self-Awareness*. New York: Praeger.

Chapman, David W., and Michael S. Green. 1996. "Teacher Retention: A Further Examination." *Journal of Educational Research* 79: 273–279.

Covey, Stephen. 1989. *The Seven Habits of Highly Effective People: Restoring the Character Ethic*. New York: Simon and Schuster.

Daniels, Harvey. 2002. *Literature Circles*. 2d ed. Portland, ME: Stenhouse.

Danielson, Charlotte. 1996. *Enhancing Professional Practice: A Framework for Teaching*. Alexandria, VA: Association for Supervision and Curriculum Development.

Darling-Hammond, Leslie, ed. 1994. *Professional Development Schools: Schools for Developing a Profession*. New York: Teachers College Press.

Dill, Vicky S., and Delia Stafford-Johnson. "Can Teachers Be Found and Certified to Teach Students At Risk?" www.altcert.org/articles.asp?article=part1&page=Articles.

Dyson, Anne Haas, and Celia Genishi, eds. 1994. *The Need for Story: Cultural Diversity in Classroom and Community*. Urbana, IL: National Council of Teachers of English.

Friere, Paulo. 1970. *Pedagogy of the Oppressed*. New York: Continuum.

Glatthorn, Allan A. 1996. *The Teacher's Portfolio: Fostering and Documenting Professional Development*. Rockport, MA: Pro>Active Publications.

Goodlad, John I. 1984. *A Place Called School: Prospects for the Future*. New York: McGraw-Hill.

Gray, John. 1999. *How to Get What You Want and Want What You Have: A Practical and Spiritual Guide to Personal Success*. New York: HarperCollins.

Hardcastle, Beverly. 1988. "Spiritual Connections: Proteges' Reflections on Significant Mentorships." *Theory into Practice* 27, 3: 201–208.

Hoffman, Charlene M. 2003. *Mini-Digest of Education Statistics*. Washington, DC: U.S. Department of Education, National Center for Education Statistics.

Knutson, Gay G. 2002. "Alternative High Schools: Models for the Future? horizon.unc.edu/projects/HSJ/Knutson.asp.

Levine, Marsha, ed. 1992. *Professional Practice Schools: Linking Teacher Education and School Reform*. New York: Teachers College Press.

Lortie, Daniel. 1975. *Schoolteacher: A Sociological Study*. Chicago: University of Chicago Press.

Mayfield, Marlys. 2001. *Thinking for Yourself: Developing Critical Thinking Skills Through Reading and Writing.* 5th ed. Fort Worth, TX: Harcourt.

McLaughlin, Maureen, and MaryEllen Vogt. 1996. *Portfolios in Teacher Education.* Newark, DE: International Reading Association.

Metzger, Margaret. 1996. "Maintaining a Life." *Phi Delta Kappan* 77, 5: 346–351.

Niday, Donna. "Beginning Again: Mentoring the Novice Teacher." Ph.D. diss., University of Iowa, 1996.

Odell, Sandra. 1990. "Support for New Teachers." In Theresa Bey and C. Thomas Holmes, eds., *Mentoring: Developing Successful New Teachers.* Reston, VA: Association of Teacher Educators.

———. 1992. "Teacher Mentoring and Teacher Retention." *Journal of Teacher Education* 43, 3: 200–204.

Palmer, Parker. 1998. *The Courage to Teach: Exploring the Inner Landscape of a Teacher's Life.* San Francisco: Jossey-Bass.

Purves, Alan C., and Joseph A. Quattrini. 1997. *Creating the Literature Portfolio.* Lincolnwood, IL: NTC Publishing Group.

"Quality Counts 2000." *Education Week* [Special Issue]. January 13, 2000: 8–163.

RoAne, Susan. 1993. *The Secrets of Savvy Networking: How to Make the Best Connections for Business and Personal Success.* New York: Time Warner.

Rogers, Shari Everts, and Kathy Everts Danielson. 1996. *Teacher Portfolios: Literary Artifacts and Themes.* Portsmouth, NH: Heinemann.

Rosenblatt, Louise M. 1978. *The Reader, the Text, the Poem: The Transactional Theory of the Literary Work.* Carbondale, IL: Southern Illinois University Press.

Salvador, Roberta. 2003. "No Dream Denied: A Pledge to America's Children." The National Commission on Teaching and America's Future. www.nctaf.org/dream/press.html.

Schön, Donald A. 1983. *The Reflective Practioner: How Professionals Think in Action.* San Francisco: Jossey-Bass.

———. 1987. *Educating the Reflective Practitioner: Toward a New Design for Teaching and Learning in the Professions.* San Francisco: Jossey-Bass.

———. 1991. *The Reflective Turn: Case Studies in and on Educational Practice.* New York: Teachers College Press.

Tannen, Deborah. 1990. *You Just Don't Understand: Women and Men in Conversation.* New York: Ballantine Books.

Tishman, Shari, David Perkins, and Eileen Jay. 1995. *The Thinking Classroom: Learning and Teaching in a Culture of Thinking.* Boston: Allyn and Bacon.

Vygotsky, Lev S. 1978. *Mind in Society: The Development of Higher Psychological Processes.* Cambridge, MA: Harvard University Press.

Westerman, Delores. 1999. "Expert and Novice Teacher Decision Making," *Journal of Teacher Education* 42: 292–305.

Wilcox, Bonita, and Lawrence Tomei. 1999. *Professional Portfolios for Teachers: A Guide for Learners, Experts, and Scholars.* Norwood, MA: Christopher-Gordon.